Progress-Monitoring Comprehension Strategy Assessments for Grades 5–6

Newmark Learning

629 Fifth Avenue • Pelham, NY • 10803

ISBN 978-1-60719-050-9

For ordering information, call Toll-Free 1-877-279-8388 or visit our Web site at www.newmarklearning.com.

Table of Contents

Grade 5	Grade 6

Introduction

Progress-Monitoring Comprehension Strategy Assessments for Grades 5-6 are a series of two-page assessments you can administer periodically during the school year to monitor your students' growth as a result of comprehension strategy instruction or intervention. Each assessment has a reading passage and five test items to measure one specific strategy. The assessments cover sixteen comprehension strategies (see Table of Contents), and there are three assessments per strategy covering a range of reading levels from Grades 5–6. Administer the level of assessment that best meets your students' needs:

Assessment Level	Administer to the Following Students
Grade 5	Students in Grade 5 reading at Levels 44–50 (S–U) Students in Grade 6 reading at Levels 44–50 (S–U)
Grade 6	Students in Grade 6 reading at Level 60 (V–X) Students in Grade 7 reading at Level 60 (V–X)

You may wish to administer assessments after completing instruction in particular strategies, or you may administer them at other appropriate times, such as the end of each grading period. These pages may be used as reading assessments or listening assessments.

Administering and Scoring the Reading Comprehension Assessments

The Grade 5 and Grade 6 Ongoing Comprehension Strategy Assessments are designed to be used primarily as reading comprehension assessments. Each assessment consists of a reading passage and five questions. Three of the questions are multiple-choice questions; the other two are short-answer questions.

Short-answer questions require students to write out their answers. Most of these responses will be one to three sentences long.

Plan for about 15–20 minutes to administer an Ongoing Comprehension Strategy Assessment, but allow more time if needed.

To Administer an Ongoing Assessment

1. Make a copy of the assessment for each student.
2. Have students write their names and the date at the top of each test page.
3. Direct students to read each passage and answer the questions that go with it.
4. For each multiple-choice question, instruct students to choose the best answer and fill in the bubble beside the answer they choose.
5. For short-answer questions, instruct students to write their responses (in phrases or complete sentences) on the lines provided.

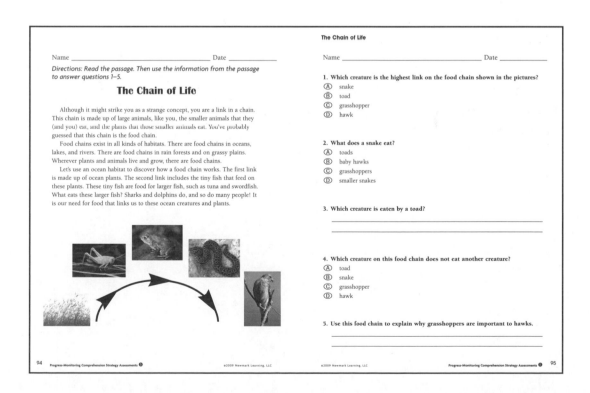

Listening Comprehension

The Grade 5 and Grade 6 Ongoing Comprehension Strategy Assessments may also be used as measures of listening comprehension. To use these assessments for listening purposes, read the passage aloud to the student(s) and have the student(s) answer the questions. The student(s) may respond by marking and writing their answers on the test page, or you may have student(s) give oral responses. If you prefer, you may use two of the three assessments for each strategy for reading comprehension and the other for listening comprehension.

To Score the Ongoing Assessment

1. Refer to the appropriate Answer Key (on pages 104–109). The Answer Key provides the letter of the correct response for each multiple-choice question. The Answer Key also provides a sample correct response for each short-answer question.

2. Mark each question correct or incorrect on the test page. You may need to interpret the student's written responses and decide whether the responses are correct, based on the sample answers in the Answer Key.

3. To find the total score, count the number of items answered correctly.

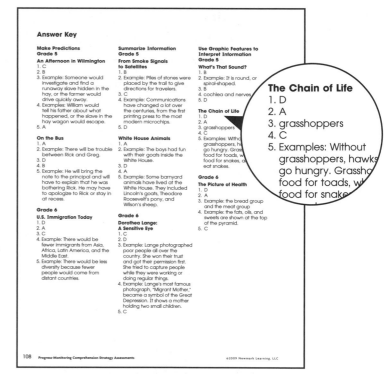

Answer Key

Make Predictions
Grade 5
An Afternoon in Wilmington
1. C
2. B
3. Example: Someone would investigate and find a runaway slave hidden in the hay, or the farmer would drive quickly away.
4. Examples: William would tell his father about what happened, or the slave in the hay wagon would escape.
5. A

On the Bus
1. A
2. Example: There will be trouble between Rick and Greg.
3. D
4. B
5. Example: He will bring the note to the principal and will have to explain that he was bothering Rick. He may have to apologize to Rick or stay in at recess.

Grade 6
U.S. Immigration Today
1. D
2. A
3. C
4. Example: There would be fewer immigrants from Asia, Africa, Latin America, and the Middle East.
5. Example: There would be less diversity because fewer people would come from distant countries.

Summarize Information
Grade 5
From Smoke Signals to Satellites
1. B
2. Example: Piles of stones were placed by the trail to give directions for travelers.
3. C
4. Example: Communications have changed a lot over the centuries, from the first printing press to the most modern microchips.
5. D

White House Animals
1. A
2. Example: The boys had fun with their goats inside the White House.
3. D
4. A
5. Example: Some barnyard animals have lived at the White House. They included Lincoln's goats, Theodore Roosevelt's pony, and Wilson's sheep.

Grade 6
Dorothea Lange:
A Sensitive Eye
1. C
2. D
3. Example: Lange photographed poor people all over the country. She won their trust and got their permission first. She tried to capture people while they were working or doing regular things.
4. Example: Lange's most famous photograph, "Migrant Mother," became a symbol of the Great Depression. It shows a mother holding two small children.
5. C

Use Graphic Features to Interpret Information
Grade 5
What's That Sound?
1. B
2. Example: It is round, or spiral-shaped.
3. B
4. cochlea and nerves
5. D

The Chain of Life
1. D
2. A
3. grasshoppers
4. C
5. Examples: Without grasshoppers, h[...] go hungry. Gras[...] food for toads, w[...] food for snakes, a[...] eat snakes.

Grade 6
The Picture of Health
1. D
2. A
3. Example: the bread group and the meat group
4. Example: the fats, oils, and sweets are shown at the top of the pyramid.
5. C

The Chain of Life
1. D
2. A
3. grasshoppers
4. C
5. Examples: Without grasshoppers, hawks[...] go hungry. Grassh[...] food for toads, w[...] food for snake[...]

Using the Results

1. Use the results of the Ongoing Comprehension Strategy Assessments to evaluate each student's understanding of the tested strategy or skill.

2. A student who understands and applies a given strategy should answer at least four of the five items correctly. A student who answers correctly fewer than four items may need additional instruction on a particular strategy.

3. Use the Scoring Chart on page 110 to keep track of students' scores on the assessments during the school year. The chart provides space for writing a student's score on each of the assessments and for noting comments relevant to a student's progress in learning a particular strategy.

Ongoing Comprehension Strategy Assessment Record

Student Name _____   Grade _____

Strategy	Test 1 Date / Score	Test 2 Date / Score	Test 3 Date / Score	Notes
Analyze Character	Date: ____ / 5	Date: ____ / 5	Date: ____ / 5	
Analyze Story Elements	Date: ____ / 5	Date: ____ / 5	Date: ____ / 5	
Analyze Text Structure and Organization	Date: ____ / 5	Date: ____ / 5	Date: ____ / 5	
Compare and Contrast	Date: ____ / 5	Date: ____ / 5	Date: ____ / 5	
Draw Conclusions	Date: ____ / 5	Date: ____ / 5	Date: ____ / 5	
Evaluate Author's Purpose and Point of View	Date: ____ / 5	Date: ____ / 5	Date: ____ / 5	
Evaluate Fact and Opinion	Date: ____ / 5	Date: ____ / 5	Date: ____ / 5	
Identify Cause and Effect	Date: ____ / 5	Date: ____ / 5	Date: ____ / 5	
Identify Main Idea and Supporting Details	Date: ____ / 5	Date: ____ / 5	Date: ____ / 5	
Identify Sequence or Steps in a Process	Date: ____ / 5	Date: ____ / 5	Date: ____ / 5	
Make Inferences	Date: ____ / 5	Date: ____ / 5	Date: ____ / 5	
Make Judgments	Date: ____ / 5	Date: ____ / 5	Date: ____ / 5	
Make Predictions	Date: ____ / 5	Date: ____ / 5	Date: ____ / 5	
Summarize Information	Date: ____ / 5	Date: ____ / 5	Date: ____ / 5	
Use Graphic Features to Interpret Information	Date: ____ / 5	Date: ____ / 5	Date: ____ / 5	
Use Text Features to Locate Information	Date: ____ / 5	Date: ____ / 5	Date: ____ / 5	

Directions: *Read the passage. Then use the information from the passage to answer questions 1–5.*

Rather Retires

On March 9, 2005, Dan Rather gave his last broadcast as the anchor of CBS News. Rather was the face and voice of *CBS Evening News* for 24 years. His first love, though, was never the news desk. More than anything, Rather loves reporting. His background as a field reporter shaped his work as an anchor.

As a child, Rather's heroes were radio newsmen. He listened to their broadcasts and noticed how their voices brought people together. He wanted to do what those newsmen did.

Rather got his big break in 1961 when Hurricane Carla headed for Galveston, Texas, and he was the only reporter in the area. During the storm, he tied himself to a tree to show how strong the wind and rain were. Rather loved being right where the news was really happening.

CBS News liked Rather's work in Galveston and soon asked him to cover the national news. He was the first to report that President John F. Kennedy had been shot and killed in November 1963. He covered the civil rights movement during the 1960s. It was a hard job. He got called names and spat on, but he wouldn't give up because he knew how important the civil rights movement was.

The TV news brought the struggle into people's homes, and his reports had to show people what black Americans were fighting for and why.

During the Vietnam War, Rather went to Vietnam and traveled with a Marine unit on its missions. He saw for himself what the soldiers went through. He also made sure Americans at home saw. Film from that time shows Rather on the ground with the soldiers as he describes what he sees.

On March 9, 1981, Dan Rather became the anchor of *CBS Evening News*. He often felt tied down by having to be in the studio at the anchor desk instead of being in the field.

Partly, Rather handled his struggles by changing how a news anchor worked. When something big happened in the world, he anchored the news from the field. He broadcast from China, Bosnia, Indonesia, and Iraq, among other places. Other anchors soon had to follow his lead. Today, anchors often travel where the news is and then broadcast from there.

Rather says he's not retiring. At age 78, Dan Rather is going back to his first love, working as a reporter.

Name _____ Date _____

1. Which sentence best describes Dan Rather?

Ⓐ He enjoys being around people.

Ⓑ He is both determined and brave.

Ⓒ He gets bored very easily.

Ⓓ He generally gets his way.

2. Why was Dan Rather such a good field reporter?

Ⓐ He understood how to tell people what they wanted to hear.

Ⓑ He felt tied down when he had to broadcast from the studio.

Ⓒ He believed that listening to the news brought people together.

Ⓓ He loved reporting the news live from the middle of the action.

3. How did Dan Rather feel about the radio newsmen he listened to as a child?

Ⓐ He admired them and their work very much.

Ⓑ He believed they had too much power over people.

Ⓒ He thought they should do more live reporting.

Ⓓ He found their broadcasts fun and entertaining.

4. Why did Dan Rather sometimes struggle with being a news anchor?

_____

_____

5. What does Dan Rather believe about how to report the news? Give one or two details from the passage to support your answer.

_____

_____

Directions: *Read the passage. Then use the information from the passage to answer questions 1–5.*

The "No Pets" Problem

Anthony Lester adored animals, but unfortunately he could not own a dog, cat, guinea pig, hamster, or even a white mouse. Anthony was allergic to animal fur.

"Mom, how about a snake?" Anthony wondered aloud.

"Sorry," said Mrs. Lester. "You know snakes eat mice."

"How about a parrot?" Anthony persisted.

"No feathers allowed," Mr. Lester said.

To every pet suggestion Anthony made, Mr. and Mrs. Lester replied "no pets" with heavy hearts. They did have some good news, though. Anthony would soon be visiting Grandpa Lester for a vacation.

Grandpa Lester lived on the west coast of Florida. Anthony loved the warm waters of the Gulf of Mexico and the sandy beaches there. He swam in the gulf and went fishing with his grandfather.

One night at bedtime, Grandfather Lester said to Anthony, "Get a flashlight from the garage while I get some snacks from the kitchen." With their supplies, the two walked out the back door and toward the beach.

At Grandpa's direction, they settled down beneath a tall palm tree. "Wait, be quiet, and be patient," said Grandpa Lester.

An hour later, Grandpa Lester's eyes lit up as he pointed down the beach. There Anthony saw an army of large loggerhead turtles climb out of the water onto the beach. They dug holes in the sand and laid eggs in the holes before heading back to the water. "Incredible!" Anthony whispered.

Grandpa Lester explained that these turtles climbed onto the beach only one night each year to lay their eggs.

At home a few days later, Anthony brought up the "no pets" problem once again.

"Just about every pet you would like has fur, or eats something with fur," Mr. Lester said.

Then Anthony told his parents about the night on the beach with the loggerhead turtles. "How about a turtle?" he nervously asked.

His parents looked at each other and grinned. "Perfect!" they replied.

Name _____ Date _____

1. **How did Anthony's parents feel when they had to keep saying "no pets"?**

(A) pleased

(B) relieved

(C) sorry

(D) impatient

2. **Why couldn't Anthony have a cat or a dog for a pet?**

(A) His apartment was too small.

(B) He was not old enough.

(C) His parents did not like animals.

(D) He was allergic to animal fur.

3. **Which sentence best describes Anthony?**

(A) He does not give up easily.

(B) He likes to whine and complain.

(C) He is used to getting his own way.

(D) He does not get along with his parents.

4. **How does Anthony feel about his grandfather? Give a detail from the story to support your answer.**

_____

_____

5. **Why did Anthony probably think that a turtle would make a better pet than a fish?**

_____

_____

Directions: Read the passage. Then use the information from the passage to answer questions 1–5.

A Hero for Working People

Just after World War II, in 1949, Poland became one of many countries in Eastern Europe ruled by the Soviet Union. But in a small Polish town called Popowo, there lived a boy who would change all that.

Lech Walesa never had an opportunity to attend college. He started work fixing cars when he was 18 and then went into the army in 1965. Two years later, he became an electrician in the Gdansk shipyards. He learned to care about his fellow workers.

Over the years, Walesa became angry that he and his friends had no rights as workers and no say in their jobs. In fact, they had no say in anything. They had to do what the communist government in the Soviet Union told them to do. Walesa tried to start a workers' union in 1976, hoping that the government would listen to their demands, but instead he was fired from his job.

That didn't stop Walesa, though. He started organizing workers' strikes and talking to people all over Poland about his concerns. Sometimes he was in danger, but he continued his efforts anyway. He was made the head of a new group for workers called Solidarity. In 1981, Lech Walesa was arrested and confined in a house far away from the cities and the workers.

Then in 1983, word reached Poland that Lech Walesa had won the Nobel Peace Prize. Now he was famous all over the world. The government was forced to take him and his workers seriously when they called for changes in Poland. Before long, political elections were held. Lech Walesa, the hero of the Polish people, was elected president of the country. Ever since then, Polish people have been able to elect their own leaders.

Name _____ Date _____

1. According to the passage, why did Lech Walesa want to start a workers' union?

Ⓐ   He wanted to become rich.

Ⓑ   He hoped it would make the government listen.

Ⓒ   He wanted to show support for communism.

Ⓓ   He lived far away from the cities and workers.

2. Which words best describe the character of Lech Walesa?

Ⓐ   reckless and foolish

Ⓑ   quiet and reserved

Ⓒ   courageous and bold

Ⓓ   greedy and self-serving

3. Why did Lech Walesa become angry about his situation?

_____

_____

4. Which detail from the passage supports the idea that Lech Walesa acted bravely?

Ⓐ   He continued talking to people even though he was in danger.

Ⓑ   He started fixing cars when he was only 18 years old.

Ⓒ   He joined the army and then became an electrician.

Ⓓ   He learned to care about his fellow workers.

5. Why was the communist government finally forced to take Lech Walesa seriously?

_____

_____

Directions: *Read the passage. Then use the information from the passage to answer questions 1–5.*

Making Yippee

Krista Thirsten lived on Zanos, the rainiest, loneliest, most boring planet in the universe. Because of her father's job, she would be a prisoner on Zanos without her Earth friends for all 365 days of one whole year.

"Think of it as a challenge," Mr. Thirsten told Krista on day 300. "I think you pass muster."

"I'll give it a try," Krista mumbled as she slumped in her chair.

"Learn to be your own best friend if no one else is around," said her father cheerfully. "We'll be home before you know it."

Krista promised her father she would try her best to enjoy Zanos, although she couldn't help but feel sorry for herself. It rained almost every minute of every day, and she had no friends on Zanos.

On the morning of day 315, something peculiar happened. The sun shone for the first time! Krista dashed outside. Beautiful blue grass that felt like cool velvet covered the field. She sprinted to the crest of a hill and rolled down, shouting, "Yippee!" in delight.

"Yipp-yeeep-yee!" she heard in response from a squeaky voice. Krista stopped and looked up as an odd-looking creature with four legs crawled over the hill toward her. It looked at Krista with its three sparkling eyes and said, "Earth person, what was that you said? It is not an Earth word I comprehend."

Krista was so surprised she didn't know what to say. The creature said, "Today is Sun Day on Zanos. This day is a special day. We who live on Zanos make friends with those from Earth, so I will be your friend."

Odd as the creature sounded and appeared, Krista smiled and became its friend for Sun Day.

By the time the sun finally went down at the end of the day, Krista had almost forgotten that she was on another planet. Now she could see the light at the end of the tunnel. She had found a new friend, and there were only forty-nine days left before she and her father would go home to Earth. Zanos wasn't such a bad place after all.

Name _____ Date _____

1. How did Krista feel at the beginning of the story?

Ⓐ   adventurous

Ⓑ   happy

Ⓒ   spoiled

Ⓓ   lonely

2. Where does this story take place?

Ⓐ   on a spaceship

Ⓑ   in a prison

Ⓒ   on another planet

Ⓓ   in a school

3. What was Krista's main problem?

Ⓐ   She did not have any friends on Zanos.

Ⓑ   She was afraid of the creatures she saw.

Ⓒ   She did not like being with her father.

Ⓓ   She had an argument with her best friend.

4. What event made Krista suddenly feel happier?

_____

_____

5. Why did Krista decide that Zanos "wasn't such a bad place after all"?

_____

_____

Name _____ Date _____

Directions: Read the passage. Then use the information from the passage to answer questions 1–5.

Double Take

Setting: *Felix and Edwin are identical twins. They were adopted by two different families as babies, but neither boy nor his adopted family knows about the other twin. Felix lives in Houston, Texas. He is on a family vacation in New York City, where Edwin lives. Edwin is on a class trip to Ellis Island. The play begins in the main building of Ellis Island, where immigrants entered the United States between 1892 and 1954. Felix and Sally are walking one way around a display of photographs in the center of a room. Edwin and Jeremy are walking around the same display in the opposite direction.*

JEREMY (*to Edwin and pointing at a photograph*): Look at that kid in the funny cap. He could be my cousin Seth on a bad clothes day!

EDWIN: That cap is not funny. That's what kids wore in 1901. Read the captions, Jeremy. Get with the history program. (*He chuckles and pushes his friend along. Then as he moves to the left he accidentally bumps into Sally and Felix Redon.*) Oh, sorry.

SALLY: No problem. (*As Sally glances up at Edwin, she looks shocked. She turns to her brother and whispers.*) Felix, do you see those two boys?

FELIX: Sure. (*When Felix sees the resemblance between himself and Edwin, he stops.*) Do you see what I see?

SALLY: I see you. I mean, two of you!

JEREMY (*in a shaky voice*): Edwin, do you see what I see?

EDWIN: It can't be. (*He slowly walks up to Felix.*) Excuse me, what's your name? (*Both boys stare at each other.*)

FELIX: Felix. Felix Redon. Who are you?

EDWIN: Edwin. Edwin Hart.

SALLY (*excited but shocked*): You even have the same voice, but Mom and Dad never said anything about a twin.

JEREMY (*to Sally*): I don't mean to pry into your family business, but how could a twin be a secret?

FELIX: Well, I was adopted when I was a baby, so my parents were not actually my first parents.

EDWIN (*gulps*): I was adopted, too! (*The boys check each other over, smiling at the thought that they may have uncovered an amazing family mystery.*) Are your parents here with you, Felix?

FELIX: They're down the hall. Let's go. (*The boys run off together, side by side.*) (*Curtain closes.*)

Name _____ Date _____

1. Where does this scene take place?

Ⓐ   in a building on Ellis Island

Ⓑ   on a boat in New York Harbor

Ⓒ   at the Statue of Liberty

Ⓓ   at a baseball game in New York

2. In this scene, who is Jeremy?

Ⓐ   Edwin's brother

Ⓑ   Sally's brother

Ⓒ   a friend of Edwin

Ⓓ   a friend of Felix

3. Which sentence best describes the plot?

Ⓐ   Ellis Island is a place that many tourists visit.

Ⓑ   People long ago dressed differently from people today.

Ⓒ   Families from different parts of the country visit Ellis Island.

Ⓓ   Twin boys discover each other while visiting Ellis Island.

4. How did Edwin meet Felix?

_____

_____

5. Why did Edwin and Felix run off at the end of the scene?

_____

_____

Name _____ Date _____

Directions: Read the passage. Then use the information from the passage to answer questions 1–5.

The Happy Camper

When Caroline and I crawled out of our tent, I groaned that my sleeping bag must have had rocks beneath it. I ached all over. Caroline, of course, had no problem at all. She was chirpy as ever and said she had slept like a baby.

"Juanita, there's nothing better than camping in the great outdoors," were her exact words to me.

Truthfully, I would rather have been in my living room, curled up on the rug, watching a DVD. Of course, Caroline could join me if she didn't mind staying indoors.

As I daydreamed about my cozy home, Caroline said she couldn't wait to have breakfast cooked over an open fire. I couldn't resist trying to rattle this happy camper just a little by asking if she'd like some tasty wild porcupine broiled over the flames.

When Caroline told me I had a sick sense of humor, she began to laugh, which got me started, too. Our laughter woke up the other girls from our club and the parent chaperones.

Caroline and I quickly decided to go wash up at the outdoor water pump, and I followed her down the path in the woods. Caroline was ahead of me, and she started to challenge me to a race when, suddenly, she stopped dead in her tracks. She turned to me with her smile wilted and her rosy cheeks gone pale.

My eyes followed Caroline's finger and the direction it pointed in. I saw the water pump several yards in front of us, and I also saw the snake curled up beside it. Caroline nodded that she was afraid of snakes when I asked her, so I patted her on the back and explained that it was a harmless milk snake. I knew that because my brother and I once had one as a pet. To tell you the truth, the snake was the first interesting thing that happened on this camping trip.

Suddenly I was smiling, beaming with excitement, and guess who won the race to the pump? Who was the happy camper now?

Name _____ Date _____

1. **Who is the narrator of this story?**

Ⓐ   Caroline

Ⓑ   Juanita

Ⓒ   a parent chaperone

Ⓓ   an outside observer

2. **What is the setting of the story?**

_____

_____

3. **Which word best describes how Caroline feels at the beginning of the story?**

Ⓐ   grumpy

Ⓑ   carefree

Ⓒ   bored

Ⓓ   homesick

4. **What is the problem at the beginning of the story?**

Ⓐ   Caroline and Juanita have different attitudes about camping.

Ⓑ   The other girls are asleep when Caroline and Juanita wake up.

Ⓒ   Caroline and Juanita cannot be friends with each other.

Ⓓ   The parent chaperones did not bring fresh water for the campers.

5. **How does Juanita's mood change by the end of the story, and why does it change?**

_____

_____

Directions: Read the passage. Then use the information from the passage to answer questions 1–5.

Getting Energy from the Sun

You probably realize that without the sun, there would be no life on Earth. Earth would most likely be a dark, frozen, lifeless piece of rock. All life on Earth depends on the sun's light and heat, but just how does the sun produce energy to create light and heat? How does the sun really work?

What is the sun?

You may already know that the sun is a star. A star is a huge ball of burning **gas** held together by **gravity**. If you could travel to the center of the sun, you would find its **core**, which is the densest part of the sun. Gravity is strongest at the core. That is where the process that produces light and heat begins.

What happens in the sun's core?

Inside the sun's core, a process called **fusion** takes place. Fusion happens when two or more parts of one thing join together to make something else. Inside the sun, atoms of hydrogen gas join together to make another gas called helium. Fusion creates **energy**. The energy then travels out of the core toward the surface of the sun.

What happens on the sun's surface?

Closer to the **surface**, the gases that make up the sun are not as densely packed as they are at the core. The energy from the core heats up the gas. Think about what happens when you heat a pot of water on the stove. The burner on the stove produces heat. The heat travels through the pot and into the water. As the water heats up, little bubbles form. Finally, the water boils and you can see and hear the bubbles. This is what happens on the sun's surface. The bubbles "burst," sending their energy into space as light and heat. In time they cool and the gas sinks back into the sun. There, the gas heats back up and forms new bubbles. Then it goes through the process of giving off energy again. Some of that energy travels 93 million miles to Earth and brings us the light and heat we need to live.

Name _____ Date _____

1. Most of the information in this passage is organized by _____.

Ⓐ comparison and contrast

Ⓑ causes and effects

Ⓒ time order

Ⓓ questions and answers

2. In paragraphs three and four, the author presents information as _____.

Ⓐ events in history

Ⓑ steps in a process

Ⓒ facts and opinions

Ⓓ problems and solutions

3. What happens inside the sun when fusion takes place?

Ⓐ Atoms of hydrogen gas join to make helium, creating energy.

Ⓑ Gravity pulls gases inside the sun together into a dense ball.

Ⓒ Energy travels out of the core toward the surface of the sun.

Ⓓ Helium gas inside the sun heats up and becomes less dense.

4. At what point does the sun release energy into space?

_____

_____

5. Why does the author use bold type in some parts of this passage?

_____

_____

_____

_____

Name _____ Date _____

Directions: Read the passage. Then use the information from the passage to answer questions 1–5.

Robot Cars Aren't Up to the Challenge

No one knew when the day began that the Grand Challenge would have no winner. No one really had any idea what would happen.

The Defense Advanced Research Projects Agency (DARPA) sponsored the race. DARPA wanted to find ways to solve the problem of building a robot that could move and navigate by itself. Many teams had been working on their bots for months. Over 100 groups wanted to enter the Challenge. Only 25 came up with working vehicles. On the morning of the race, only 15 vehicles lined up at the start.

On the day of the Grand Challenge, team members checked their bot cars over one last time. They tested the brakes, the steering, and the tires. The course stretched 142 miles through the Mojave Desert. The robots had to find their way along rocky paths, up hills, and along steep ridges. They had to get through open desert and across paved highways. Once they left the starting area, their teams could not help them. The prize for completing the course was $1 million.

At last someone signaled that the first bot should begin the course. That's when the real fun started! One bot started the race by slamming into a wall. One bot's brakes locked up in the starting area, and it couldn't go anywhere. Next, one went off in the wrong direction and would not come back. One flipped upside down. Another just drove around in circles, getting in the way of all the other cars.

A few vehicles got out of the start area. The first traveled 1.2 miles before it got "scared" by a bush and drove off the course. Another got about the same distance before slamming into a fence. A bot that traveled 5.2 miles stopped for no reason on a steep hill. A mile and a half down the road, a bot got stuck on a rock. The vehicle that traveled the farthest went 7.4 miles before it ran into a small ridge and its wheels caught on fire.

DARPA hoped the Challenge would result in many new ideas and solutions for building robots. By 2015, the army plans to replace soldiers with bots on some dangerous missions, and DARPA is working to help meet that goal. Though the Challenge seemed like a failure, DARPA and the teams learned a lot. Now DARPA has to take the best ideas from each robot car and put them together. The teams want to help too when they return for the next Grand Challenge.

Name _____ Date _____

1. What is the main type of structure the author uses to organize this passage?

Ⓐ   comparison and contrast

Ⓑ   order of importance

Ⓒ   problems and solution

Ⓓ   cause and effect

2. Which sentence from the passage gives the best clue to the way the text is organized?

Ⓐ   Many teams had been working on their bots for months.

Ⓑ   DARPA wanted to find ways to solve the problem of building a robot that could move and navigate by itself.

Ⓒ   Next, one went off in the wrong direction and would not come back.

Ⓓ   On the morning of the race, only 15 vehicles lined up at the start.

3. What happened just before the race began?

Ⓐ   Over 100 groups decided to enter the Challenge.

Ⓑ   Each team checked its robot's parts and systems carefully.

Ⓒ   One robot car's brakes locked up in the starting area.

Ⓓ   The army asked DARPA to develop working robot cars.

4. What information does the author provide in the third paragraph?

_____

_____

5. What was the author's goal in paragraphs four and five?

_____

_____

Name _____ Date _____

Directions: Read the passage. Then use the information from the passage to answer questions 1–5.

Music from Steam

Imagine a big piano or organ that can be heard for miles and miles and that rides in a wagon or on a boat. If that big musical instrument is powered by steam, it's a calliope!

What is a calliope?

A calliope (pronounced kuh-LIE-uh-pee) is a musical instrument powered by steam. It has 32 to 44 metal keys, which control large whistles. Steam blows through the whistles. It takes one person to play the keys, but one other person has to add fuel to keep making steam. The steam is very hot, so the keys get hot, too. Playing the calliope is hard work!

Where were calliopes played?

In the late 1800s, there were calliopes all over America. Some were on steamboats that traveled up and down the rivers, such as the Mississippi. People always knew when the steamboat was coming because they could hear the calliope playing! Calliopes were also played in circuses. The circus arrived in a parade of wagons, and the calliope often rode in the last wagon. It played so loudly that even people in nearby towns could hear it. Children came running when they heard the calliope.

Where are they now?

The first calliope was built in Worcester, Massachusetts, in 1855, and they soon started appearing everywhere. But in the 1900s steam power started to fade out, and calliopes began to disappear. Now there are only 14 left in the world. A few steamboats still have them. They are still very loud, and people still love to hear them!

Music from Steam

Name _____ Date _____

1. Most of the information in this passage is organized by _____.
Ⓐ problems and solutions
Ⓑ comparison and contrast
Ⓒ questions and answers
Ⓓ cause and effect

2. The function of the second paragraph in this passage is to _____.
Ⓐ describe what a calliope is
Ⓑ tell how calliopes were invented
Ⓒ give information about steamboats
Ⓓ express the author's opinion of calliopes

3. According to the second paragraph, a calliope can best be described as _____.
Ⓐ an old steamboat
Ⓑ a steam-powered organ
Ⓒ an alarm bell
Ⓓ an instrument in a wagon

4. According to the third paragraph, where were calliopes usually found?

_____

_____

5. Where are the calliopes now?

_____

_____

Directions: *Read the passage. Then use the information from the passage to answer questions 1–5.*

Elephant Songs

At first glance, it might not seem as though elephants and whales have much in common. Elephants live on land in Africa and Asia. Whales live in the world's oceans.

Still, whales and elephants are both large mammals. Both live in family groups made up of females and young males, while adult males tend to live alone. Both animals take care of their young. Now researchers have found another way in which they are alike. Elephants and whales use the same kinds of sounds to "talk" to each other.

Scientists have been listening to "whale songs" for many years. Whales communicate using low-frequency sounds. These "infrasonic" sounds are too low for people to hear. Whales use the sounds to tell each other many things. Some sounds warn of danger. Other sounds mean that one group has found food. Whales send out sounds when they are hurt or need help. Females call males to mate. Whales also use ultrasonic sounds, which are too high for people to hear. The high sounds help them determine where they are in the ocean.

In 1990, a scientist named Katy Payne discovered that elephants use infrasonic sounds, too. Payne spent the first part of her career studying whales and already knew a lot about their sounds. One day Payne was standing next to the elephant cage at a zoo. She felt as if the air around her was vibrating a little. She wondered if the elephants were making infrasonic calls. She and two other scientists tested her idea. Sure enough, the elephants were making the sounds.

Many people have since studied elephant communication. Like whales, elephants use low-frequency sounds to talk to each other "long-distance." They use sounds as warning calls and to pass on information. Unlike whales, elephants have limited space to live in. Their calls help them coordinate their movements and send mating calls at the right times.

While whales' calls travel through water, elephants' calls must travel through the air. Most whale calls can be heard up to 6 miles away. Through the air, most elephant calls travel up to 6 miles. But they also travel through the ground. A call makes the earth vibrate. Elephants feel these vibrations through their feet and "hear" the messages. Sounds traveling as ground waves go much farther than sounds traveling through air.

Name _____ Date _____

1. In what way are whales and elephants different?

Ⓐ Elephants are large mammals.

Ⓑ Whales live in family groups.

Ⓒ Elephants have limited space to live in.

Ⓓ Whale songs are too low for people to hear.

2. In what way are whales and elephants alike?

Ⓐ Their calls travel through the ground as vibrations.

Ⓑ They "hear" through their bodies as well as their ears.

Ⓒ Some of their calls are too high for people to hear.

Ⓓ They like to stay in contact with others of their kind.

3. Unlike whales, elephants _____.

Ⓐ send signals through the air

Ⓑ take care of their young

Ⓒ use sounds to warn of danger

Ⓓ make sounds that can be heard for several miles

4. Whales and elephants both use infrasonic sounds to communicate what kinds of information?

_____

_____

5. What did Katy Payne discover that no one knew before?

_____

_____

Name _____ Date _____

Directions: Read the passage. Then use the information from the passage to answer questions 1–5.

Kayaks

Today many people like to go kayaking for fun. For the Inuit people, kayaks were once an essential part of life. The Inuit, once called "Eskimos," live in the Arctic region. They used kayaks and boats called umiaks for traveling, carrying goods, hunting, and fishing.

Inuit kayaks had wooden frames with sealskins stretched over them to make the boats watertight. These kayaks were long, slender, and low in the water. Their shape made them easy to paddle quickly and quietly. They were also light enough for one person to carry easily.

Inuit kayaks had a cockpit just behind the center of the boat. Kayakers sat in the cockpit and stretched their legs out below the deck. They used a double-bladed paddle and paddled from side to side. Sometimes a kayaker wore a waterproof jacket and hooked the bottom of the jacket to the rim of the cockpit to keep water out.

The Inuit stretched rawhide thongs along the decks of their kayaks. They could slide their weapons, such as harpoons, or other tools under the thongs. The thongs kept the weapons in place and easy to reach.

The umiak was similar to the kayak in some ways. It too had a wooden frame covered with animal skins. But umiaks were open boats. They were larger, wider, and higher than kayaks. They could hold up to 30 people as well as gear. Umiaks were used mainly for transporting people and goods. When the Inuit traveled, the women rowed the umiaks while the men followed in their kayaks.

Today most of the Inuit use motorboats. A few people build umiaks as a hobby. But kayaking has become a popular sport. Most modern kayaks are made of plastic or fiberglass and are heavier than Inuit kayaks.

Many kayaks still have a cockpit where paddlers sit on a plastic seat. As the Inuit did, paddlers stretch their legs out under the deck. Today, a waterproof spray skirt attaches to the cockpit to keep the water out. Kayakers still use double-bladed paddles. Most of them are made of metal or plastic now, though, not wood. Instead of rawhide thongs, strong elastic bands stretch across the deck. Kayakers store things like extra paddles or backpacks under the bands.

Progress-Monitoring Comprehension Strategy Assessments ❺

Kayaks

Name _____ Date _____

1. **In what way were umiaks like kayaks?**
   (A)   They were open boats.
   (B)   The Inuit used them for hunting and fishing.
   (C)   They held up to 30 people.
   (D)   They had wooden frames covered by animal skins.

2. **An Inuit kayaker's waterproof jacket served much the same purpose as the modern kayak's _____.**
   (A)   fiberglass shell
   (B)   elastic bands
   (C)   spray skirt
   (D)   plastic seat

3. **Inuit kayaks were different from umiaks in that they _____.**
   (A)   were used to transport goods
   (B)   were long, slender, and low
   (C)   could be either paddled or rowed
   (D)   often were paddled by women

4. **In what way are the elastic bands on modern kayaks similar to the rawhide thongs on Inuit kayaks?**

   _____

   _____

5. **How are today's kayaks different from the kayaks built by the Inuit? Give at least two differences.**

   _____

   _____

Name _____ Date _____

Directions: Read the passage. Then use the information from the passage to answer questions 1–5.

Are Hybrid Cars Safe?

Most cars run on gas alone. Hybrid cars run on both gas and a rechargeable electric motor. The electric motor saves money and energy. Because of high gas prices and concerns about having enough oil, hybrid cars have become quite popular. They are known to be just as safe to drive as regular cars. Some people even think that they are safer than regular cars. This is because hybrids tend to be small, quick, and easy to handle. However, hybrid cars may be a cause for concern to emergency workers and car mechanics.

Sometimes when a car is in an accident, emergency workers need to cut through the car to save people inside. The batteries in hybrid cars are 40 times more powerful than those in regular cars. This means there is a strong electric current running through the car. Rescue workers must shut down the electric motor before cutting into the metal parts of the car. If they don't, they could receive a severe electric shock.

The electric current in hybrid cars can also be dangerous for car mechanics. Mechanics who work on regular cars must learn new safety steps for working on hybrids. One step is shutting down the electric motor before starting their work. If they do not do this, they too could run the risk of getting an electric shock.

As hybrid cars become more widely used, carmakers may find new ways to address these safety concerns. Until then, emergency workers and car mechanics should always take safety measures when working with hybrid cars.

Are Hybrid Cars Safe?

Name _____ Date _____

1. **Based on the passage, which is one way that hybrid cars and regular cars are alike?**
   Ⓐ They both run on gasoline alone.
   Ⓑ They are both considered safe to drive.
   Ⓒ Their batteries produce the same amount of electrical current.
   Ⓓ They are both dangerous for car mechanics.

2. **According to the first paragraph, how are regular cars and hybrid cars different?**

   _____

   _____

3. **In what way are hybrid cars different from regular cars?**
   Ⓐ They have larger engines.
   Ⓑ They have more towing power.
   Ⓒ They have stronger batteries.
   Ⓓ They have more room for passengers.

4. **When the author describes the batteries in hybrid cars and regular cars in the second paragraph, is this a comparison or a contrast? Why?**

   _____

   _____

5. **Why are hybrid cars more dangerous to car mechanics than regular cars are?**
   Ⓐ They can cause electric shocks.
   Ⓑ They are more likely to explode.
   Ⓒ They often cause acid burns.
   Ⓓ They are more likely to break apart.

Name _____ Date _____

Directions: *Read the passage. Then use the information from the passage to answer questions 1–5.*

Etna Blows Its Top

On July 17, 2001, Mount Etna blew its top. Lava and ash started to pour out of the mountain from four different places. Both the tourist area and cable car at the mountain were closed. Visits to Mount Etna were restricted to government officials and scientists only. But officials were not taking any chances with people's lives.

Mount Etna is located on the island of Sicily, which is part of Italy. It is Italy's highest peak at about 10,958 feet (3,340 meters). It is also Europe's tallest active volcano. The first known eruption of Mount Etna took place around 475 B.C. Many eruptions have occurred since then. Since 1971, there have been at least 14 small eruptions from the sides of the mountain.

The people who live near Mount Etna seem to have become used to the eruptions. Local farmers still grow crops, such as grapes and olives, on the mountainside. The people on the island might be happier if this volcano became dormant and stopped erupting. But there is no sign of that happening yet.

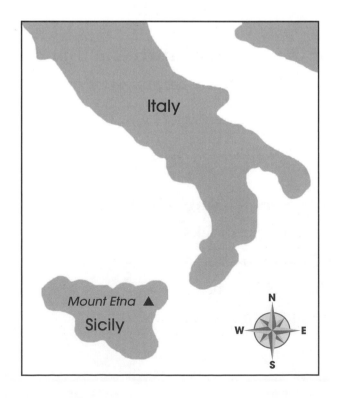

Name _____ Date _____

1. **What can you conclude from the fact that scientists and government officials went to Mount Etna on July 17, 2001?**
   Ⓐ They knew there was no danger.
   Ⓑ They lived near the mountain.
   Ⓒ They wanted to study the volcano.
   Ⓓ They had become used to eruptions.

2. **What can you conclude from the fact that the tourist area and cable car at Mount Etna were closed in July 2001?**

   _____

   _____

3. **From the information in the passage, you can conclude that _____.**
   Ⓐ Mount Etna will continue to erupt for many years to come
   Ⓑ the people of Sicily live in constant danger
   Ⓒ one of the three volcanoes on Sicily erupts every day
   Ⓓ lava from Mount Etna is helpful to the farmers

4. **What can you tell about Sicily from this passage?**
   Ⓐ It has a large population.
   Ⓑ No one lives there for very long.
   Ⓒ It used to be part of Greece.
   Ⓓ Tourists like to visit Mount Etna.

5. **How do the people of Sicily feel about Mount Etna? Use clues from the passage to support your answer.**

   _____

   _____

Name _____ Date _____

Directions: Read the passage. Then use the information from the passage to answer questions 1–5.

Solving Problems

Calvin's friend Sonya is running for class president. She orders Calvin to vote for her, threatening she will no longer walk to school with him if he doesn't. Calvin enjoys walking to school with Sonya. But he prefers to cast his vote for the person with the best ideas for the job. One of the other candidates is Danita. Calvin thinks that she has some excellent ideas about what she would do as class president.

What can Calvin do? He comes up with three possible choices. One, he can vote for Sonya so he can continue to walk to school with her. Two, he can vote for Danita but keep his vote a secret from Sonya. Three, he can tell Sonya he thinks it is important for each person to make a choice based on who presents the best ideas.

Next, Calvin thinks about what will happen as a result of each choice. If he votes for Sonya, he will not be voting for the candidate he feels has the best ideas. If he votes for Danita but keeps his vote a secret, he will not feel comfortable around Sonya. If he tells Sonya he believes a person should choose the best candidate, he will be telling the truth about a subject important to him.

Calvin decides that the third choice is the best one for him. Now he has to figure out how to put his plan into action. He decides to talk to Sonya when they walk to school the next day.

The next morning, Calvin explains what he has been thinking and what he has decided. In response, Sonya says, "You know, you're right. You should make up your own mind. I shouldn't make your choice for you just because we're friends. If I come up with some great ideas, though, I hope you will vote for me."

The election is only a week away. Calvin decides to listen carefully to everything Sonya, Danita, and the other candidates have to say. Now he knows he can vote with confidence. He also knows that he will still enjoy his walks to school with Sonya.

Name _____ Date _____

1. **At the beginning of this passage, how does Calvin feel about Sonya and Danita as candidates for class president?**

Ⓐ He plans to vote for Sonya.

Ⓑ He thinks Danita is the best candidate.

Ⓒ He does not like either of the candidates.

Ⓓ He is sure that Sonya will win.

2. **Write a detail from the passage that helped you answer question 1.**

_____

_____

3. **What conclusion about Calvin can be drawn from this passage?**

Ⓐ He tries to be honest with others.

Ⓑ He will do whatever it takes to keep Sonya as a friend.

Ⓒ He thinks that school elections are unfair.

Ⓓ He often makes rash decisions without thinking first.

4. **Write a detail from the passage that helped you answer question 3.**

_____

_____

5. **From the passage, what can you conclude about Calvin and Sonya?**

Ⓐ They have not been friends for very long.

Ⓑ They have worked together on many school projects.

Ⓒ Both believe that people have to make their own choices.

Ⓓ Both of them think that class president is a silly job.

Name _____ Date _____

Directions: Read the passage. Then use the information from the passage to answer questions 1–5.

Let's Take a Closer Look

Have you ever looked through a microscope or seen a picture of a small object that has been magnified? The objects that you saw looked larger because of special magnifying lenses. A magnifying lens is made by grinding a piece of glass into a curved shape. The curves cause things seen through the glass to look larger.

How long have people used magnifying lenses? Ancient Romans used them to focus the sun's rays as well as to magnify things. Lenses did not become widely used until the 1200s when people began wearing eyeglasses. As people began to use magnifying lenses more, they began to experiment with them. This led to the invention of the microscope.

The first microscopes were not very strong. They only magnified things about ten times their normal size. Then in the 1600s, a man named Anton van Leeuwenhoek from Holland taught himself how to grind small lenses to create very strong magnification. He made a stronger microscope. Using his new microscope, he was the first person to see living things within a drop of water. He could even see and describe tiny bacteria.

In England, a man named Robert Hooke was also doing work with magnification. He used Leeuwenhoek's work as a foundation for his work. Hooke began with Leeuwenhoek's microscope and improved it. He also noticed that water contained tiny living things. After that, the microscope did not change much for the next 100 years or so. Then, in the 1800s, an American named Charles Spencer began making even better microscopes.

The microscope has led to important medical discoveries. Much of what we know today about bacteria, cells, and curing disease we learned by using microscopes.

Name _____ Date _____

1. **Based on the passage, you can conclude that _____.**
   - (A) Hooke's microscopes were stronger than Spencer's
   - (B) Hooke's lenses were the finest lenses ever made
   - (C) Leeuwenhoek's work helped Robert Hooke's work
   - (D) Leeuwenhoek was smarter than Hooke

2. **What can you conclude from the information in the second paragraph?**
   - (A) Lenses became more important when eyeglasses were invented.
   - (B) Before 1200, people did not need to magnify things.
   - (C) The ancient Romans were very skilled at making different kinds of lenses.
   - (D) No one needed eyeglasses or lenses until the 1200s.

3. **You can conclude from the third paragraph that before Leeuwenhoek, no one really knew that _____.**
   - (A) glass could be made in different shapes
   - (B) lenses could be used to focus sunlight
   - (C) lenses helped some people see things better
   - (D) there were living things in a drop of water

4. **What conclusion can you draw about the contribution Anton van Leeuwenhoek made to the field of medicine?**

   _____

   _____

5. **What evidence from the passage supports the conclusion that the invention of microscopes has improved people's lives?**

   _____

   _____

Name _____ Date _____

Directions: Read the passage. Then use the information from the passage to answer questions 1–5.

Two Sisters

After the Civil War ended in 1865, an ex-slave named Henry Beard Delany worked hard to become a bishop of the Episcopal Church. He and his wife Martha then raised ten children. They gave their children good educations. They also taught them an important rule: "Your job is to help somebody."

Two of the Delany children lived by that rule and became famous. They were Sarah "Sadie" Louise and Annie Elizabeth "Bessie" Delany. Sadie and Bessie became teachers in their home state of North Carolina. Later, they moved together to Harlem in New York City. Both went to Columbia University. Sadie earned degrees in science and education. Bessie became a dentist. Sadie was the first African American home economics teacher in New York City. Bessie became the second African American dentist to earn a license in New York.

Sadie and Bessie never forgot the family motto. Through their jobs, they helped many people in Harlem.

The Delany sisters were remarkable in several ways. They lived very long lives. They often defied rules and laws that were unfair. They also lived through many historic events. For example, their father had been a slave who lived through the Civil War. Both sisters lived to see the Civil Rights Act become law 100 years later. This act made it unlawful to treat any American unfairly. The Delany sisters also knew many famous people in Harlem.

Why do people today know of the Delany sisters? In 1991, a reporter from the *New York Times* wrote an interesting article about the sisters. The article led to a book, *Having Our Say: The Delany Sisters' First 100 Years*. It became a best seller. Later, it was turned into a play and a film.

In 1995, Bessie died at the age of 104. Sadie wrote a second book when she was 107. She lived to the grand old age of 109. Both sisters certainly had long and exciting lives.

Two Sisters

Name _____ Date _____

1. What is the author's main purpose in writing this passage?

_____

_____

2. Which sentence from the passage best indicates the author's view of the Delany sisters?

Ⓐ Later, they moved together to Harlem in New York City.

Ⓑ The Delany sisters were remarkable in several ways.

Ⓒ They also lived through many historic events.

Ⓓ The Delany sisters also knew many famous people in Harlem.

3. Which sentence in the last paragraph sums up the author's views on the Delany sisters?

_____

_____

4. Which sentence from the passage states the author's opinion?

Ⓐ Bessie became a dentist.

Ⓑ Sadie earned degrees in science and education.

Ⓒ In 1995, Bessie died at the age of 104.

Ⓓ In 1991, a reporter from the *New York Times* wrote an interesting article about the sisters.

5. The author probably mentioned that both sisters became teachers because he wanted to _____ .

Ⓐ explain why they moved to New York City

Ⓑ prove that they were very smart

Ⓒ show that they really did help others

Ⓓ suggest that they could have done better

Name _____ Date _____

Directions: Read the passage. Then use the information from the passage to answer questions 1–5.

Pigs or Plants?

Hawaii is a land of beautiful plants, but it is also a place with a great number of endangered plants. Pigs are the reason for this problem.

People from Europe brought wild pigs to Hawaii. Before long, there were many pigs running wild on the islands. They ate many native Hawaiian plants. They also dug in the underbrush, and this digging uprooted delicate plants. It also made the soil better for alien plants to grow. Some of the new plants became a threat to Hawaii's native plant life.

There has been another side effect of the pigs' digging. When it rains, pools of water form where the pigs have dug. Mosquitoes lay their eggs in the pools. Because of the pigs, mosquitoes have become a huge problem. Some of them carry diseases that affect native birds and other animals.

Hawaiians have been trying to stop the spread of wild pigs. They have put up fences and have encouraged hunting and trapping. But many people have spoken out against hunting the pigs. They feel that since people are responsible for bringing the pigs to Hawaii, they should not kill them now that they are there.

Hawaiians must decide whether their forests are more important than the pigs. To save the native plants and many of the native animals as well, the pigs must go. It is now a race against time. Twenty-five percent of Hawaii's forests have disappeared. Will the Hawaiians choose the pigs or the plants?

Name _____ Date _____

1. **The author's main purpose in the first four paragraphs of this passage is to _____.**
   - Ⓐ inform readers about Hawaii's problem
   - Ⓑ entertain readers with a funny story
   - Ⓒ persuade readers to visit Hawaii
   - Ⓓ explain how readers can help Hawaii

2. **How does the author's purpose change in the last paragraph?**
   - Ⓐ She tries to tell a story to entertain readers.
   - Ⓑ She stops trying to persuade and just informs.
   - Ⓒ She tries to persuade readers to think a certain way.
   - Ⓓ Her purpose does not change.

3. **What is the author's point of view on the wild pigs?**
   - Ⓐ She thinks they should not be hunted.
   - Ⓑ She thinks they are an important part of the Hawaiian ecosystem.
   - Ⓒ She thinks they are a threat to Hawaii's native plants.
   - Ⓓ She thinks they should be tamed.

4. **Why does the author mention mosquitoes in this passage?**

   _____

   _____

5. **What details reveal the author's point of view about the wild pigs?**

   _____

   _____

Name _____ Date _____

Directions: Read the passage. Then use the information from the passage to answer questions 1–5.

Island of Mystery

In the Pacific Ocean, far from any other lands, lies a mysterious place called Easter Island. This strange island is covered with many huge statues carved from stone. The statues are very old, and no one knows exactly why they were made. They look like odd-shaped heads, but they are really whole carved bodies. The earth has built up around them over time, so the bodies of most of the statues are buried up to their necks.

The island also has many stone tablets with writing on them. Many people have tried to understand the writing, but so far no one knows what it means. Maybe someday someone will figure it out, and then perhaps we'll finally learn what the statues mean.

There have been people living on Easter Island for almost 2,000 years. No one knows for sure where the first islanders came from. The island is thousands of miles west of Chile and is now part of that country. But most scientists think the first people came from the opposite direction. They think small boats from other Pacific islands landed on Easter Island long ago.

Ecology of an Island

Forests are an important part of our world. Easter Island is an example of what happens when forests are cut down. Long ago, Easter Island had lots of palm trees and thousands of people. But the people cut the trees down to build boats and houses and to make space for their statues. After a while, the trees were all gone. Soon the people couldn't build boats, and this meant they couldn't go fishing. Without trees, the soil began to wash away. No one could grow food, and people began to starve. In a short time, only a few hundred people remained.

In our time, Easter Island has hardly any trees. It is covered with grass. The palm trees that used to be there are now extinct. This island is a good example of what happens when people do not take care of the forests.

Name _____ Date _____

1. **The author's purpose in the first passage is to _____.**
   - (A) give information about Easter Island
   - (B) compare Easter Island with other islands
   - (C) persuade the reader to visit Easter Island
   - (D) explain how to locate Easter Island

2. **The author of the first passage seems to think that Easter Island is _____.**
   - (A) dangerous
   - (B) pitiful
   - (C) fascinating
   - (D) shameful

3. **The author's main purpose in the second passage is to _____.**
   - (A) entertain the reader
   - (B) teach a lesson
   - (C) explain how to make something
   - (D) give directions

4. **According to the author of the first passage, what is one of the mysteries of Easter Island?**

   _____

   _____

5. **In the second passage, what is the author's view of what the people did on Easter Island?**

   _____

   _____

Name _____ Date _____

Directions: Read the passage. Then use the information from the passage to answer questions 1–5.

Two Native American Peoples: The Iroquois and the Zuni

Hundreds of Native American tribes lived in North America long before the Europeans arrived. The Iroquois League and the Zuni tribe were two of these groups. They were also two of the most interesting. Although they lived in different parts of North America, they had much in common.

Most of the people of the Iroquois League came from tribes, such as the Mohawk, that lived in what is now New York State. The Iroquois lived mainly in large wooden houses called longhouses. The houses were quite roomy and comfortable. In each longhouse, more than one family lived as a group. The group was run by women. The most important part of Iroquois life was farming. This was also run by women. The women grew corn, beans, and squash. The men were hunters and warriors. Fifty male chiefs, or sachems, ruled the Iroquois League. But those men were chosen by the women.

The Zuni tribe lived in the Southwest along the Zuni River. Their lands were near the border between what are now Arizona and New Mexico. Unlike the Iroquois, the Zuni built houses of clay, or adobe. Each family had its own house. Like the Iroquois, farming lay at the center of Zuni life. Zuni women cared for gardens near their villages. They grew corn, chilis, herbs, and spices. The Zuni men were skilled hunters. Zuni men also became chiefs and religious leaders called shamans. Long ago, Zuni women made beautiful clay pots, for which the Zuni are still famous.

Today, the Iroquois people live on eight reservations set aside for them. These lands are in New York, Canada, and Oklahoma. Most of these lands are not where their Iroquois ancestors lived. The reservation set aside for the Zuni in New Mexico, however, is different. It includes land that Zuni ancestors lived on long ago. The Zuni people still live in adobe houses. But the Iroquois no longer live in wooden longhouses.

Two Native American Peoples: The Iroquois and the Zuni

Name _____ Date _____

1. Which sentence from the passage states an opinion?

Ⓐ Hundreds of Native American tribes lived in North America.

Ⓑ The Iroquois League and the Zuni tribe were two of these groups.

Ⓒ They were also two of the most interesting.

Ⓓ They lived in different parts of North America.

2. Which sentence from the second paragraph states an opinion?

Ⓐ Most of the people of the Iroquois League came from tribes, such as the Mohawk, that lived in what is now New York State.

Ⓑ The Iroquois lived mainly in large wooden houses called longhouses.

Ⓒ The houses were quite roomy and comfortable.

Ⓓ In each longhouse, more than one family lived as a group.

3. Write a sentence from the second paragraph that states a fact. Tell how you know it is a fact.

_____

_____

4. Write a sentence from the third paragraph that states an opinion. Tell how you know it is an opinion.

_____

_____

5. Which sentence states an opinion?

Ⓐ Women were the most important people in every tribe.

Ⓑ Today, the Iroquois live on eight reservations.

Ⓒ The Zuni reservation is located in New Mexico.

Ⓓ Iroquois reservations are in New York, Canada, and Oklahoma.

Directions: Read the passage. Then use the information from the passage to answer questions 1–5.

Having It Both Ways

One day in 1920, a boy walked into Christian K. Nelson's ice cream and candy store. He asked for a chocolate bar. Then he changed his mind and asked for an ice cream sandwich. Ice cream and chocolate are both wonderful treats, Nelson reasoned. Wouldn't it be great to find a way to put them together?

Nelson began experimenting with ways to make a chocolate and ice cream treat. His idea was to coat a slab of ice cream with melted chocolate. Then he would cool it so the chocolate hardened into a thin skin. Nelson was not very good at making chocolate, though. He had little luck until he got a tip from a candy salesman. The salesman explained that candy bar makers changed the amount of cocoa butter in their chocolate based on the filling inside.

With this advice in mind, Nelson worked long and hard until he found a formula that worked. Then he started selling the chocolate-covered ice cream bars to his customers. The bars were a huge hit. Nelson's creations were delicious, and people loved them. He went into business making and selling his new treat, which he named "Eskimo Pie."

Before long, Eskimo Pies were being sold all over the country. Customers were eating more than one million a day! Nelson himself became rich and famous, thanks to a lot of hard work. That little boy who could not make up his mind was a great help, too.

Having It Both Ways

Name _____ Date _____

1. Which sentence from the passage states an opinion?

Ⓐ   One day in 1920, a boy walked into Christian K. Nelson's ice cream and candy store.

Ⓑ   He asked for a chocolate bar.

Ⓒ   Then he changed his mind and asked for an ice cream sandwich.

Ⓓ   Ice cream and chocolate are both wonderful treats.

2. Which sentence from the second paragraph states an opinion?

Ⓐ   Nelson began experimenting with ways to make a chocolate and ice cream treat.

Ⓑ   Then he would cool it so the chocolate hardened into a thin skin.

Ⓒ   Nelson was not very good at making chocolate, though.

Ⓓ   The salesman explained that candy bar makers changed the amount of cocoa butter in their chocolate based on the filling inside.

3. Which sentence from the third paragraph states a fact?

Ⓐ   With this advice in mind, Nelson worked long and hard until he found a formula that worked.

Ⓑ   Nelson's creations were delicious, and people loved them.

Ⓒ   The bars were a huge hit.

Ⓓ   He went into business making and selling his new treat, which he named "Eskimo Pie."

4. Write a sentence from the last paragraph that states a fact. Tell how you know it's a fact.

_____

_____

5. Write a sentence from the last paragraph that states an opinion. Tell how you know it's an opinion.

_____

_____

Name _____ Date _____

Directions: Read the passage. Then use the information from the passage to answer questions 1–5.

A Monument to the Country

Each year, more than one million people travel to South Dakota to see Mount Rushmore. It is a popular place to visit. Despite its popularity, there are differing views among Americans toward Mount Rushmore.

Most monuments are built to remind us of a great person, event, or belief. The faces of Thomas Jefferson, Abraham Lincoln, Theodore Roosevelt, and George Washington are carved into Mount Rushmore. These are four of America's most respected presidents. Their faces remind many people of the proud history of the United States. This history should be honored. Many people view Mount Rushmore as a monument to democracy.

Other people view Mount Rushmore as a symbol of broken promises to Native Americans. Mount Rushmore stands in the Black Hills of South Dakota, which was once the sacred land of the Lakota Sioux. In the 1800s, the U.S. government promised the Lakota that they could live on this land forever. Then someone discovered gold in the Black Hills. After that, the promise was broken. The government's actions were shameful.

In 1939, another monument was started close to Mount Rushmore. It is a carving of Crazy Horse, a famous Sioux warrior. The monument is still not finished.

It took 14 years to complete Mount Rushmore. Although the work was very dangerous, not a single worker died. This was a great achievement. The work was done during the Great Depression. Some people thought it was a waste of money. They were wrong. It was well worth the cost to honor four great leaders of the United States.

Name _____ Date _____

1. Which sentence states a fact about Mount Rushmore?

Ⓐ   It is a great monument.

Ⓑ   It is a popular spot to visit.

Ⓒ   It cost too much money to build.

Ⓓ   It should not have been built in the Black Hills.

2. Which sentence from the passage states an opinion?

Ⓐ   "Each year, more than one million people travel to South Dakota to see Mount Rushmore."

Ⓑ   "The faces of Thomas Jefferson, Abraham Lincoln, Theodore Roosevelt, and George Washington are carved into Mount Rushmore."

Ⓒ   "These are four of America's most respected presidents."

Ⓓ   "Many people view Mount Rushmore as a monument to democracy."

3. Write a sentence from the third paragraph that expresses an opinion.

_____

_____

4. Write a sentence from the third paragraph that states a fact.

_____

_____

5. Which sentence from the last paragraph states an opinion?

Ⓐ   "It took 14 years to complete Mount Rushmore."

Ⓑ   "Although the work was very dangerous, not a single worker died."

Ⓒ   "The work was done during the Great Depression."

Ⓓ   "It was well worth the cost to honor four great leaders of the United States."

Name _____ Date _____

Directions: Read the passage. Then use the information from the passage to answer questions 1–5.

Amphibian Population Declining: Scientists Concerned

What's happening to the world's frogs, toads, and other amphibians? Amphibians are cold-blooded, and they tend to live near water. Thousands of species of amphibians live all over the world. But studies show that their numbers have declined very suddenly. Hundreds of species now face extinction. Scientists aren't sure why this is happening, but they are worried. They fear that it may signal trouble that could affect other living things on Earth, including people.

Some scientists blame pesticides for these problems. Farmers use these poisons to keep bugs from eating their crops. Amphibians have very thin skin. They absorb poisons quickly. Pesticides cause problems with the way frogs develop. For example, the back legs of some frogs do not grow long enough. Their short legs make it hard for them to swim. Also, some frogs can't breed. Fewer babies mean fewer frogs.

Amphibians are also disappearing, though, in places where pesticides are not used. Some people blame the problem on loss of habitat. For example, people have been cutting down the rain forests in South America for the past 25 years. The amphibians that once lived there now have no place to live. Amphibians have also been forced out by cities and towns. As more people move into an area, they use up more of the land.

Pollution may also be hurting amphibians. Air pollution allows more radiation from the sun to reach Earth. Once again, amphibians' thin skin hurts them. The radiation gets through their skin more easily than it does the skin of other animals.

Scientists warn that big problems with the environment would affect amphibians first. Because of this, the death of so many amphibians is like a red flag to the rest of us. We must figure out what is killing Earth's amphibians before it's too late.

Progress-Monitoring Comprehension Strategy Assessments ❺

Amphibian Population Declining: Scientists Concerned

Name _____ Date _____

1. **What effect do some pesticides have on frogs?**
   - Ⓐ They cause the frogs' skin to become thinner.
   - Ⓑ They change the way that frogs behave.
   - Ⓒ They cause frogs to develop abnormally.
   - Ⓓ They damage the brains of baby frogs.

2. **What happens when frogs cannot breed normally?**
   - Ⓐ Their population begins to decline.
   - Ⓑ Other animals can catch them more easily.
   - Ⓒ Certain species begin to grow faster.
   - Ⓓ They get sick more often.

3. **What characteristic of amphibians makes them less able than other animals to deal with certain changes in their environment?**
   - Ⓐ their need to be near water
   - Ⓑ the fact that they are cold-blooded
   - Ⓒ their breeding habits
   - Ⓓ the thinness of their skins

4. **How does the growth of cities and towns affect frogs and other amphibians?**

   _____

   _____

5. **Why are scientists so concerned about the sudden decline in amphibian populations?**

   _____

   _____

Name _____ Date _____

Directions: Read the passage. Then use the information from the passage to answer questions 1–5.

Explaining Earthquakes

Somewhere in the world an earthquake occurs every day. Some of them are very small and can hardly be felt. Other quakes, like the one that occurred in the Indian Ocean in December 2004, are huge. People thousands of miles away feel the earth shake. Large earthquakes cause terrible destruction, but what are they and why do they occur?

Earthquakes happen because of sudden bursts of energy released from below Earth's surface. Earth's outer crust is divided into a number of huge pieces called tectonic plates. These plates "float" on the molten rock below the surface. A fault line, or crack, occurs where two plates meet.

Earth's tectonic plates are always moving. Sometimes they move against each other along a fault line. The grinding of one plate against another causes stress in the rock. The stress builds and builds until the rock cannot hold anymore. It bends, stretches, and finally cracks. When the rock around a fault cracks, it releases energy. The energy travels through the rock in waves. These waves cause the earth to shake.

The size of an earthquake depends partly on how much strain has built up along the fault line. If the rock has been under stress for a long time, then a large earthquake may occur. Sometimes a number of small earthquakes occur along a fault in a short time. These relieve stress on the rock and, as a result, make a large earthquake less likely.

When the ground shakes under buildings, roads, and bridges, it can cause much damage. Buildings and roads may crack or collapse. Sometimes gas lines break, and this can result in huge fires. Water lines burst and power lines fall.

Earthquakes can lead to other disasters, too. Mud or rock slides can bury buildings, roads, and people. Volcanoes may erupt. Perhaps the worst result of an earthquake is a tsunami. Tsunamis are series of huge waves that can wash away whole towns and change coastlines. In fact, the earthquake in the Indian Ocean in 2004 did not cause much damage itself. It was the tsunami caused by the earthquake that really did the damage. The giant wave wiped out hundreds of villages and killed over 200,000 people.

Name _____ Date _____

1. Fault lines occur because _____.
   Ⓐ   Earth is made up of separate plates that run into each other
   Ⓑ   rocks below the surface of Earth crack
   Ⓒ   Earth's tectonic plates float on a layer of liquid rock
   Ⓓ   earthquakes cause the ground to shake and crack

2. What is the effect of tectonic plates grinding against each other?
   Ⓐ   Energy waves travel through Earth's crust.
   Ⓑ   New fault lines form along the edges of the plates.
   Ⓒ   Stress builds up in the rock where the plates meet.
   Ⓓ   Molten rock rises through cracks to Earth's surface.

3. Which of these was caused by the earthquake that struck in the Indian Ocean in 2004?
   Ⓐ   A new fault line was formed.
   Ⓑ   Rock slides buried thousands of people.
   Ⓒ   Several small volcanoes erupted.
   Ⓓ   A tsunami wiped out hundreds of villages.

4. What happens when too much stress causes the rock along a fault line to crack?

   _____

   _____

5. According to the passage, what problems can earthquakes cause other than the damage caused by ground movement?

   _____

   _____

Directions: Read the passage. Then use the information from the passage to answer questions 1–5.

Mount St. Helens

In 1979, more than half a million people visited Mount St. Helens. It was a favorite place for fishing, hiking, and camping. Few of these visitors knew that an active volcano was nearby. A volcano is a mountain built from the rising, or eruption, of melted rock from under the surface of the earth.

Scientists began observing Mount St. Helens closely in the 1930s. They studied the vegetation in the area. By studying the plants, they saw signs that lava flows had covered that area during the 1800s. In 1975, a scientific report said that an eruption might happen very soon. Then, in 1978, another report gave more details about what would happen if Mount St. Helens erupted. These reports helped the government get ready to respond to what was to come.

On May 18, 1980, Mount St. Helens erupted. Over 230 square miles of forest burned. The eruption also caused a large earthquake. As a result, the entire north face of the mountain dropped away. The earthquakes and explosions continued for almost two months.

Since the eruption, the area around Mount St. Helens has been left untouched. This allows geologists and other scientists to study the area. They can look at how the plants and animals responded after the land was destroyed by an active volcano.

Name _____ Date _____

1. **More than half a million people visited Mount St. Helens in 1979 because they wanted to _____.**

   Ⓐ   see the volcano

   Ⓑ   watch an earthquake

   Ⓒ   study the vegetation

   Ⓓ   go fishing, hiking, and camping

2. **How did scientists know that lava flows covered the area near Mount St. Helens in the 1800s?**

   Ⓐ   They studied old photographs.

   Ⓑ   The interviewed old-timers in the area.

   Ⓒ   They studied the vegetation.

   Ⓓ   They read journals from that time.

3. **Why was the government prepared to respond to the eruption of 1980?**

   _____

   _____

4. **What caused the north face of Mount St. Helens to drop away?**

   Ⓐ   a large earthquake

   Ⓑ   erosion of the land over time

   Ⓒ   people hiking on the volcano

   Ⓓ   the burning forest

5. **Why do scientists want Mount St. Helens to be left untouched?**

   _____

   _____

Name _____ Date _____

Directions: Read the passage. Then use the information from the passage to answer questions 1–5.

Picture This!

Photographs are part of your everyday life. You see them almost everywhere. In the early 1800s, there were no photographs. Can you imagine a world without photographs?

The first photograph was made in 1826 by a Frenchman named Joseph Niépce. It was called a "heliograph" because the images were made by exposure to sunlight.

In 1839, the Frenchman Louis Daguerre created a new kind of photo called a "daguerreotype." It took only 30 minutes to create a picture in black and white. These pictures became very popular. More important was the fact that for the first time, people, places, and events could be preserved in images.

Photography developed quickly after that. In 1841, William Talbot of England invented a way to print pictures from a "negative." We still do that today. In 1888, the Kodak company made the first camera for people to buy. It cost $25. By 1900, Kodak's cardboard "Brownie" camera was selling for one dollar!

Many changes in photographic equipment took place during the 1900s. A color film was invented in 1904. The flashbulb was first used in 1925. In 1947, Edwin Land invented the Polaroid camera which produced instant pictures. The first digital camera was introduced in 1989. It enabled people to take pictures and display them on computers.

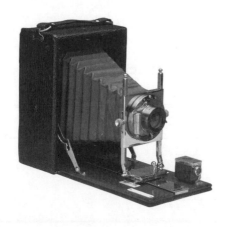  

Name _____ Date _____

1. What is the stated main idea of the first paragraph?

Ⓐ Photographs are seldom seen.

Ⓑ No one can imagine a world without pictures.

Ⓒ Photography had not been invented in the early 1800s.

Ⓓ A man named Joseph Niépce made the first photograph.

2. What would be another good title for this passage?

Ⓐ "The Development of Photography"

Ⓑ "A Man Named Niépce"

Ⓒ "Important French Investors"

Ⓓ "The Kodak Company"

3. Write a detail from the passage supporting the idea that many changes in photographic equipment were made during the 1900s.

_____

_____

4. What is the main idea of the third paragraph?

_____

_____

5. If the author wanted to add that the Leica camera was invented in 1925, in which paragraph would this detail belong?

Ⓐ paragraph 3

Ⓑ paragraph 4

Ⓒ paragraph 5

Ⓓ paragraph 6

Directions: Read the passage. Then use the information from the passage to answer questions 1–5.

Mollusks

Many animals have internal skeletons. Some creatures, such as insects, have skeletons on the outside. Animals in a third group carry their skeletons around as shells. They live inside their shells as if they were caves, and their shells protect them. These creatures, called mollusks, include clams, oysters, snails, and others.

How do these soft creatures make such strong homes for themselves? Mollusks are covered by a thick layer of skin called a mantle. This mantle oozes out layers of lime, a rocklike material. These layers are smooth and shiny, and sometimes they are colored, too. The layers overlap like the shingles on a roof, which makes them stronger and harder to break. These smooth, shiny layers are called mother-of-pearl.

Some mollusks, such as snails, have one shell. They are called univalves. Others, such as clams and oysters, have two shells and are called bivalves. Bivalves eat by opening their shells and letting water pass through. The water brings tiny animals and plants for them to feed on, and it brings more lime for their shells.

Sometimes the water brings a grain of sand or a small chunk of shell. This grit hurts the mollusk like a speck of dirt hurts your eye. A mollusk will coat the piece of grit with mother-of-pearl. That is how pearls are made. Clams and even snails make pearls, but oyster pearls are the most beautiful. Divers collect them, and people buy them to wear as jewelry.

Mollusks can be found in oceans, in rivers, and on land. When they die, many of them leave behind beautiful shells.

Name _____ Date _____

1. Which would be another good title for this passage?

(A) "So Many Skeletons"

(B) "Animals That Live in Shells"

(C) "Snails and Tails"

(D) "How to Make a Pearl"

2. What is the stated main idea of the first paragraph?

(A) Many animals have internal skeletons.

(B) Some creatures, such as insects, have skeletons on the outside.

(C) Mollusks include clams, oysters, and snails.

(D) Some animals, called mollusks, carry their skeletons around.

3. Write a sentence that tells the main idea of the second paragraph.

_____

_____

4. Write a detail from the passage supporting the idea that many kinds of mollusks are beautiful.

_____

_____

5. Suppose the author wants to add this sentence to the passage:
Most univalves have one foot that they can use to move themselves around.
In which paragraph does this sentence fit?

(A) paragraph 1   (B) paragraph 2

(C) paragraph 3   (D) paragraph 4

Name _____ Date _____

Directions: Read the passage. Then use the information from the passage to answer questions 1–5.

Time Zones

If you live in California, by the time you get up in the morning your cousin in New York may be eating lunch. This isn't because people in California sleep late. It's because the sun rises later in California than it does in New York. This is why the different areas of the United States are split into five standard time zones.

Before 1883, each city or town decided on its own time. Most places used some form of a solar clock. The sundial is one type of solar clock. It tells time by casting shadows around a dial as the sun moves across the sky. Another type of solar clock is the heliochronometer. Because the sun's height in the sky changes depending on where you are, the time in different towns varied a great deal. But people didn't travel that much so it wasn't a problem.

As people began to travel by railroad, it became more important to know the exact time in a certain place. That's when the U.S. government created five standard time zones across the country. Soon, many other countries created standard time zones as well.

The clocks around most of the world are now synchronized. This makes it easier for people to communicate with each other. With a time-zone map and a clock, you can find out what time it is anywhere. And when you travel, you'll always know what time it is in the next town, without having to look at a sundial!

Progress-Monitoring Comprehension Strategy Assessments ❻   ©2009 Newmark Learning, LLC

Name _____ Date _____

1. Which sentence best states the main idea of the passage?

(A)   In 1883, each city set its own time.

(B)   Time zones make traveling and communication easier.

(C)   California and New York are in different time zones.

(D)   Railroads made travel easier.

2. Which detail from the first paragraph explains why the United States is split into time zones?

_____

_____

3. Which sentence states the main idea of the second paragraph?

_____

_____

4. Which detail supports the idea that it became more important to know the exact time in a certain place?

(A)   Most of the clocks around the world are now synchronized.

(B)   People in California like to sleep late.

(C)   Your cousin in New York may be eating lunch when you're eating breakfast.

(D)   People began traveling long distances by railroad.

5. Which detail explains why times varied from town to town when people used heliochronometers to tell the time?

(A)   The sun's height in the sky changes depending on where you are.

(B)   People didn't travel much so it wasn't a problem.

(C)   The U.S. government created five standard time zones.

(D)   With a time-zone map and a clock, you can tell the time anywhere.

Name _____ Date _____

Directions: Read the passage. Then use the information from the passage to answer questions 1–5.

An Experiment with Light

"I see the light" is an expression that means "I understand." But is it actually possible to see light? Light is a form of energy that comes from the sun or other sources. Light travels in invisible waves called light waves. If you know how to look for one, you can discover a rainbow in an otherwise invisible light wave.

What you need:
- clear glass half-filled with water
- sheet of white paper

What to do:
1. Away from a window, hold up the clear glass half-filled with water. You won't see anything unusual.
2. Now place the glass near a window or on a windowsill so that a beam of light shines through it. You should see a rainbow.
3. Hold the white paper under the rainbow. The colors will become brighter and clearer. Look for seven colors.

How it works:
When a beam of light (a light wave) passes through the clear glass half-filled with water, the light bends because it changes speed. The water acts like a prism. The light in the beam bends again as it leaves the glass. The bending of light two times causes the light in the beam to separate. In science, this bending of light is called refraction. Each separate band of light is a color of the rainbow, and every rainbow has seven colors. From the top band to the bottom band, the colors are red, orange, yellow, green, blue, indigo, and violet. You can remember these colors by using the name ROY G BIV.

An Experiment with Light

Name _____ Date _____

1. **What is the first step in this experiment?**

    _____

    _____

2. **To make a rainbow, which step should come next?**
    (A)   Place a piece of paper underneath the glass.
    (B)   Hold the glass where there are no sunbeams.
    (C)   Place the glass near a window or on a windowsill.
    (D)   Fill a clear glass with water.

3. **What should you do in step 3?**

    _____

    _____

4. **When you see a rainbow on the paper, you should _____.**
    (A)   fold the paper
    (B)   look for seven colors
    (C)   write ROY G BIV
    (D)   tape the paper down

5. **This experiment would probably not be successful on a cloudy day because _____.**
    (A)   the glass could fill up with rain
    (B)   light does not bend when the air is cool
    (C)   light travels in invisible waves
    (D)   there would not be enough sunlight

Directions: Read the passage. Then use the information from the passage to answer questions 1–5.

Ben Franklin

Have you ever been caught in a thunderstorm? If so, then you know how scary the rain, thunder, and lightning can be. Imagine how frightening these storms were to people in the early 1700s. In those days, people had no understanding of lightning at all. Ben Franklin grew up during those times.

In 1718, 12-year-old Ben worked as an apprentice, or trainee, in his brother James's printing shop. In 1728, he opened his own printing office in Philadelphia. Three years later, he founded the city's first public library. Franklin continued in the printing business until 1748. It was in 1752 that he turned his attention to electricity and lightning.

Many people of his time believed that lightning was a strange and punishing force sent from heaven. Ben Franklin thought otherwise. He believed that lightning was a form of electricity. He set out to prove it.

One stormy night, he gathered a small piece of metal, a kite, string, and a metal key. He attached the piece of metal to the top of the kite. Then he tied the string to the kite. Next, he secured the key near the bottom of the string. With help from his son William, he launched the kite into the dark sky. Lightning struck the piece of metal at the top of the kite. It traveled down the string to the key. Franklin touched the key and there was a spark. He had proved that lightning was a form of electricity. Later, he invented the lightning rod. This device, which is still used today, protects buildings from lightning.

Name _____ Date _____

1. When did Ben Franklin introduce the first public library?

Ⓐ   before he opened a printing office in Philadelphia

Ⓑ   in the beginning of the 1730s

Ⓒ   at the end of the 1740s

Ⓓ   after his lightning experiment

2. What did Ben Franklin do before he opened his own printing office?

_____

_____

3. In his experiment, what did Ben Franklin do just before he tied the string to the kite?

Ⓐ   He turned his attention to electricity and lightning.

Ⓑ   He secured the key near the bottom of the string.

Ⓒ   He attached the metal piece to the top of the kite.

Ⓓ   He set out to prove lightning was a form of electricity.

4. What was the last thing to happen in Ben Franklin's experiment?

Ⓐ   There was a spark.

Ⓑ   Franklin touched the key.

Ⓒ   Lightning struck the metal piece.

Ⓓ   The key was secured to the string.

5. What did Ben Franklin do after his experiment with the kite?

_____

_____

Directions: Read the passage. Then use the information from the passage to answer questions 1–5.

Westward We Go!

In 1843, about 1,000 people from the eastern United States moved to the West. They drove their wagons along a route called the Oregon Trail. The trip was 2,000 miles long and very hard. It took about six months. One in ten people died along the way from accidents or diseases caused by unclean conditions.

First, settlers had to plan their departure date. If they left too early in the spring, there would not be enough grass for their animals to eat. If they left too late, they would have to travel in cold, winter weather at the end of their trip. Then, the settlers had to make a list of needed supplies. A family of four would need to take about 1,000 pounds of food with them. After all, there weren't any fast-food restaurants along the way. Third, settlers needed to decide what sort of animals would pull the wagon. Mules were faster than oxen, but oxen were gentler and easier to handle. Most travelers chose oxen. Finally, settlers had to load up their sturdy wagons and start out on the trail.

Once on the trail, the settlers had a daily routine. They would wake up before sunrise, hook the oxen to the wagon, cook breakfast, and then start moving. In the evening they would stop around six o'clock, set up camp, and then make dinner. Before they could cook, they had to collect fuel for the fire. Usually this fuel was dry buffalo waste, which burned well and was easy to find. They went to sleep by nine o'clock, and at five in the morning, the whole process started over again.

Name _____ Date _____

1. **According to the passage, what did settlers have to do first before traveling west?**
   - (A) Locate the Oregon Trail.
   - (B) Buy wagons and oxen.
   - (C) Plan their departure date.
   - (D) Wake up before sunrise.

2. **What was the second step in planning for the Oregon Trail?**
   - (A) making a list of needed supplies
   - (B) choosing what animals to take
   - (C) loading the wagon
   - (D) packing food

3. **Why did settlers have to decide what type of animals to travel with before loading their wagons?**

   _____

   _____

4. **Once on the trail, what did most settlers do every day before they had breakfast?**
   - (A) Set up a new camp.
   - (B) Hook the oxen to the wagon.
   - (C) Pack 1,000 pounds of food.
   - (D) Collect some dry fuel.

5. **On the trail, why did settlers have to collect dry buffalo waste before making dinner?**

   _____

   _____

Name _____ Date _____

A New Fin for Fuji

Fuji didn't have a flat tire, exactly, but it was a tire company that came to her rescue when she was in trouble.

Fuji is a dolphin at the Okinawa Churaumi Aquarium in Japan. A few years ago, Fuji became very ill. She had a disease that was causing her tail to rot away. Veterinarians decided that they could save Fuji but not her tail.

After a veterinarian operated on Fuji, the dolphin became healthy again. But now she had a new challenge. It was difficult for her to swim. She swam much slower than before, and she could no longer jump out of the water—not even a little bit.

The veterinarian contacted a friend who worked at a tire company. He asked if the company could create a rubber fin for Fuji. It was an unusual request, but the people at the tire company agreed to try.

The company made ten fins that did not work. Some were too heavy, and some did not fit properly. Finally the company made a fin that seemed just the right weight, but there was still a major problem. Fuji refused to wear it.

Fuji's keepers did not give up. They let Fuji wear the fin for 20 minutes at a time. After five months she became accustomed to swimming with it. But then, something even better happened. Fuji used her new fin to jump out of the water. That was a big day for Fuji, her keepers, and the people at the tire company.

She's been swimming and jumping ever since.

Name _____ Date _____

1. **What other animals are you likely to see at the Okinawa Churaumi Aquarium?**

   Ⓐ bears

   Ⓑ sharks

   Ⓒ elephants

   Ⓓ horses

2. **A veterinarian saved Fuji's life by _____.**

   Ⓐ giving her medicine

   Ⓑ changing her diet

   Ⓒ calling a tire company

   Ⓓ removing her tail

3. **What does a dolphin need its tail to do?**

   _____

   _____

4. **Which detail from the passage supports the inference that people at the tire company really wanted to help Fuji?**

   Ⓐ They made ten fins that did not work.

   Ⓑ It was an unusual request.

   Ⓒ A vet asked the company to create a rubber fin.

   Ⓓ Fuji's keepers did not give up.

5. **Why was rubber a good material to use for Fuji's new fin?**

   _____

   _____

Name _____ Date _____

Directions: Read the passage. Then use the information from the passage to answer questions 1–5.

The Statue of Helios

In the year 305 B.C., the Greek island of Rhodes was attacked. An army of 40,000 soldiers tried to conquer Rhodes, but Rhodes did not fall. After nearly a year of conflict, the invading army gave up the fight and departed from the island.

The people of Rhodes were sure they had won the war with the help of Helios, the sun god. They decided to build a statue of Helios to stand near their harbor. It would greet ships from other lands as they sailed to Rhodes.

The huge statue took 12 years to build. It had an iron frame covered with bronze, which came from the losing army's war machines. The statue stood on a stone base. From the top of Helios's head to his feet, the statue was 110 feet tall. Experts believe that Helios held a fiery torch in his right hand.

For 56 years, the huge Helios looked out over the sea—until a strong earthquake struck in 226 B.C. The statue snapped at the knees and crashed to the ground.

An Egyptian king offered money to rebuild the statue, but the people of Rhodes said no. They believed the statue fell because the god Helios did not like it. The people did not want to offend Helios again.

In a way, though, the statue of Helios lives on. One of the modern world's most famous statues is a reminder of the Colossus of Rhodes. The Statue of Liberty stands just a few feet taller than the ancient Helios, and she too holds a torch. From her spot in New York Harbor, the Statue of Liberty greets ships from other lands as they sail toward the shore.

Name _____ Date _____

1. When the invading army departed from Rhodes, what did they leave behind?

Ⓐ   war machines and weapons

Ⓑ   a statue of Helios

Ⓒ   fiery torches

Ⓓ   an Egyptian king

2. Why did it take 12 years to build the statue of Helios?

_____

_____

3. The weakest part of the statue of Helios must have been its _____.

Ⓐ   head

Ⓑ   neck

Ⓒ   knees

Ⓓ   feet

4. About how tall is the Statue of Liberty?

Ⓐ   60 feet

Ⓑ   120 feet

Ⓒ   200 feet

Ⓓ   250 feet

5. How can you tell that the people of Rhodes respected and feared the sun god Helios? Use details from the passage to support your answer.

_____

_____

Name _____ Date _____

Directions: Read the passage. Then use the information from the passage to answer questions 1–5.

Where the Buffalo Roam

For centuries, Native Americans of the Great Plains relied on wild buffalo herds for their food, shelter, and tools. In 1865, more than 12 million buffalo lived on the Great Plains. But then more and more settlers moved west. By 1890, most of these animals were gone. There were only 750 buffalo left. Fortunately, the number of buffalo has grown since then.

The animal that we call buffalo is also called American bison. Today there are about 80,000 of these big, shaggy animals in the United States. They live in parks and reserves. One herd of free-ranging buffalo lives in Yellowstone National Park. "Free-ranging" means that the animals are allowed to roam throughout the park. This is their natural way of life. Many people hope that this herd will continue to grow.

Some cattle ranchers who live near Yellowstone do not like having the buffalo there. They worry that the buffalo could come onto their land and make their cattle sick. Because of this, the government has slaughtered more than 3,500 buffalo. But many people do not believe the buffalo can actually pass diseases to cattle. In 2003, a law was passed to make it harder for the government to kill buffalo.

The buffalo once were the center of many Native Americans' way of life. They were the source of most of the things that these Native Americans needed to live. Protecting the buffalo is important. It preserves part of our natural history.

Name _____ Date _____

1. You can infer that buffalo live in parks and reserves so that _____.

Ⓐ   they will not have to travel much

Ⓑ   they have protection while their numbers grow

Ⓒ   it is easier for people to see them

Ⓓ   they do not hurt people who want to watch them

2. You can infer that millions of buffalo disappeared in the late 1800s because _____.

Ⓐ   Native Americans hunted them

Ⓑ   they caught a disease from cattle

Ⓒ   herds of buffalo moved away

Ⓓ   they were killed by settlers

3. Why are there more buffalo now than there were in 1890?

_____

_____

4. From the third paragraph of this passage, you can tell that _____.

Ⓐ   many people thought the government was wrong to slaughter buffalo

Ⓑ   ranchers value the buffalo herd more than their own cattle

Ⓒ   thousands of buffalo have been moved away from Yellowstone

Ⓓ   the buffalo carry diseases that can be harmful to humans

5. Why would cattle ranchers living near Yellowstone National Park disagree with the last two sentences in the passage?

_____

_____

Name _____ Date _____

Directions: *Read the passage. Then use the information from the passage to answer questions 1–5.*

Mushrooms

What do you think of when you see or hear the word "fungus"? A fungus (plural, "fungi") is a sort of plant, but it does not produce seeds or flowers. There are about 100,000 different kinds of fungi. They include mushrooms, toadstools, and puffballs.

Unlike green plants, fungi cannot make their own food. They also cannot move around, as animals do, to find food. As a result, fungi live off other plants as parasites, or they take food from decaying plant matter, such as dead trees. Many kinds of fungi are helpful because they break down dead plants. Others, such as the bracket fungi, are harmful because they kill trees.

If you walk in the woods, especially when the ground is damp, you may see many kinds of mushrooms and other fungi. Some kinds of mushrooms can be eaten. Fairy ring mushrooms, for example, are often used to flavor soup. Chanterelles, morels, and elephant ear mushrooms are also edible. They are cooked and served with many different kinds of foods.

Other kinds of mushrooms should not be eaten. They are poisonous. One of the most toxic is the death cap. It usually grows under oak and beech trees. Yellow staining mushrooms, earth balls, and the red-capped fly agaric are also poisonous and should be avoided.

Many kinds of mushrooms are difficult to identify. Some that are poisonous look much like those that are safe to eat. Thus, it is best to remember two rules about mushrooms: (1) Do not eat any mushrooms you are not absolutely sure about, and (2) ask an expert before you nibble on a mushroom.

Name _____ Date _____

1. **What kind of mushrooms probably taste best? Give a detail from the passage to support your answer.**

    _____

    _____

2. **Which detail from the passage best supports the judgment that eating some mushrooms could be fatal to people?**
    - Ⓐ One type of mushroom is named elephant ear.
    - Ⓑ One of the most toxic is called death cap.
    - Ⓒ Some kinds of fungi break down dead plants.
    - Ⓓ Some mushrooms grow under oak and beech trees.

3. **Which is the best reason to think that fungi are an important part of the natural world?**
    - Ⓐ Many kinds of fungi can be eaten.
    - Ⓑ Some fungi grow only under beech or oak trees.
    - Ⓒ Many kinds of fungi are hard to identify.
    - Ⓓ Some fungi break down dead plants.

4. **Suppose you are walking in the woods and are very hungry. You see some brown mushrooms growing under a tree. What should you do?**
    - Ⓐ Take the mushrooms home and cook them.
    - Ⓑ Don't eat any of the mushrooms.
    - Ⓒ Eat only the tops of the mushrooms.
    - Ⓓ Use the mushrooms to flavor a soup.

5. **What is the best reason for you to avoid eating any kind of fungi you see in the woods?**

    _____

    _____

Directions: Read the passage. Then use the information from the passage to answer questions 1–5.

Reconstruction

Between 1865 and 1877, Congress made an effort to rebuild the war-torn South after the Civil War. This period was called Reconstruction.

President Lincoln wanted the North and South to be one nation again. Lincoln insisted that the South free all the slaves and return to the Union. He wanted to make it as easy as possible for the South to rebuild.

Sadly, Lincoln was killed just after the war and his ideas were not followed. Vice President Andrew Johnson became president. He tried to follow Lincoln's ideas, but he was not successful.

Some people in the North wanted to punish the South and not help to rebuild it. Congress passed laws that made it very hard for people in the South.

Though the slaves were freed, people in the South passed laws against former slaves. These laws kept former slaves from voting, owning land, or going to school. Laws were also passed to keep them from working in many jobs.

Some people went from the North to the South to make money and gain power. They were called carpetbaggers. These people had only their own interests at heart. They were not really trying to help the South but wanted to become rich quickly. To do so, they took advantage of many Southerners. People in the South became very angry at these people from the North. This anger lasted for many decades after the war.

Reconstruction

Name _____ Date _____

1. **Which of these is a judgment you could make about the first paragraph?**

   (A) Life in the South was not strongly affected by the Civil War.

   (B) Most of the homes in the South were not destroyed.

   (C) After the Civil War, Congress had an important job.

   (D) Land in the South was worth more after the Civil War.

2. **Which of these is a judgment you could make about the second paragraph?**

   (A) Lincoln was very angry with the South for starting the war.

   (B) Lincoln was trying hard to bring the country back together.

   (C) Lincoln wanted to punish the people in the South.

   (D) Lincoln had not thought much about what would happen after the war.

3. **Which is a judgment you could make about the fifth paragraph?**

   (A) Most former slaves led better lives after the Civil War.

   (B) Many greedy people moved to the South to make money.

   (C) People in the South were wrong to pass laws against former slaves.

   (D) Former slaves in the South were able to work and go to school.

4. **Had President Lincoln lived longer, how do you think he would have felt about what happened during Reconstruction?**

   _____

   _____

5. **On what information from the passage do you base your judgment?**

   _____

   _____

Directions: Read the passage. Then use the information from the passage to answer questions 1–5.

Astronauts

Astronauts are people who travel beyond Earth's atmosphere. When the U.S. space program began in 1959, there were only seven trained astronauts. Today, there are more than 100 astronauts. However, becoming an astronaut is still very hard.

Every astronaut must have a college degree. Many of them have a graduate degree, or advanced degree. Degrees in math and science are all helpful for astronauts. Astronauts must also be very healthy. People who are in less than perfect health can become very ill from space travel. Even people who pass all of these tests and complete the training may not become astronauts. There are only a small number of openings. More than 4,000 people apply for every 20 astronaut spots.

Some people think that they should be allowed to travel in space even if they are not trained astronauts. In Russia, there is already a space program that offers space flight to civilians. People from all over the world apply to this program. They pay thousands of dollars just to go through the long review process. They take a ten-day health exam that is very strict. They also go through space-flight tests. For the few people who are chosen, the average cost to go into space is $20 million! The Russian Space Agency promotes the review process as if it were an adventure vacation.

Perhaps one day, taking a trip into space will be as normal as taking a car trip. For now, it's still a rare and costly event.

Name _____ Date _____

1. Which of these is a judgment you could make based on the second paragraph?

Ⓐ Becoming an astronaut in the U.S. space program is not easy.

Ⓑ Too many people want to become astronauts.

Ⓒ The U.S. space program is not very popular.

Ⓓ There are no openings in the U.S. space program right now.

2. Which detail from the passage supports the judgment that U.S. astronauts are smart people?

Ⓐ More than 4,000 people apply for 20 spots.

Ⓑ They study math and science.

Ⓒ Many of them have advanced degrees.

Ⓓ They have to be healthy.

3. Which of these judgments is supported by details in the third paragraph?

Ⓐ Russia has the best astronauts in the world.

Ⓑ Most people have too much money to spend.

Ⓒ The Russians like space travel more than anyone else does.

Ⓓ Space travel is one of the most exciting things you can do.

4. What statement from the passage supports the judgment that the Russian Space Agency wants to make money?

_____

_____

5. Do you think it is a good idea to make astronauts take health exams? Give at least one fact from the passage to support your answer.

_____

_____

Name _____ Date _____

Directions: Read the passage. Then use the information from the passage to answer questions 1–5.

An Afternoon in Wilmington

It was a beautiful day in 1848 when William Keen and his father drove their wagon into Wilmington, Delaware. The Keen family had recently moved to the area from Vermont. While the wagon was being filled with supplies, Mr. Keen suggested that William take a walk. "Wilmington is a fine place, son," he said. "Explore a little bit and meet me back here."

William walked past houses and shops until he got to the courthouse. Voices and people streamed out of the building as a handsome couple walked down the steps. Buzzing with excitement, a crowd of people followed the couple.

The two people were Thomas Garrett and his wife. Mr. Garrett had been on trial. Slave owners had used an old law from 1793 to sue for money they had lost when their slaves ran away. They claimed that Mr. Garrett ran the busiest station on the Underground Railroad and had helped many slaves escape.

William listened to people talk about Mr. Garrett. They strongly supported him and his efforts to help runaway slaves. They did not think the $5,400 fine was fair, and they hoped the laws would soon change. They talked about a famous runaway slave that Mr. Garrett had helped. Her name was Harriet Tubman. She returned to the South many times to help other slaves escape, often with Mr. Garrett's help.

As William watched Mr. and Mrs. Garrett walk down the street, he noticed a wagon filled with hay. A farmer tipped his hat from the driver's seat when the Garretts passed by, and Mr. Garrett tipped his hat back to the farmer. Thomas Garrett stopped at the back of the wagon for a minute and then moved on.

William walked past the wagon, too. He stopped suddenly because he thought he saw the hay shake and quiver. His heart raced, but he dared not call attention to the farmer. Instead, he turned quickly and walked back through town.

Progress-Monitoring Comprehension Strategy Assessments ❺

Name _____ Date _____

1. What will William most likely do next?

Ⓐ   He will tell the farmer to move his wagon.

Ⓑ   He will call the police.

Ⓒ   He will go back to his father.

Ⓓ   He will talk to Mr. Garrett.

2. When Mr. Keen told William to take a walk in Wilmington, you could predict that _____.

Ⓐ   Mr. Keen would get into trouble

Ⓑ   William would find some adventure

Ⓒ   Mr. Keen would be arrested

Ⓓ   William would go straight to the courthouse

3. What would most likely happen if William called attention to the farmer and his hay wagon?

_____

_____

4. Write a sentence predicting an event that would probably happen soon if this story continued.

_____

_____

5. When William rejoins his father, they most likely will _____.

Ⓐ   return home with their supplies

Ⓑ   go and find Mr. Garrett

Ⓒ   try to catch the farmer with the hay wagon

Ⓓ   pay the fine of $5,400

Directions: Read the passage. Then use the information from the passage to answer questions 1–5.

On the Bus

After breakfast, Rick quickly put on his coat and grabbed his backpack. He sprinted outside just as the school bus pulled up at the corner. As he made his way to the only empty seat, Rick noticed Greg Ranier sitting across the aisle. Rick's stomach knotted up.

Rick sat low in his seat and turned his face toward the window, but Greg had already spotted him.

"If it isn't the boy genius," Greg said in a mocking tone. "I'll bet you've got all your homework done like a good boy!" Just then Greg yanked Rick's backpack out of his hands and laughed. "Now I've got your homework—all that hard work, and nothing to show for it."

Fuming, Rick looked around. Greg and his friends were laughing and elbowing one another, but no one else seemed to notice what had happened. But then Rick caught a glimpse of the bus driver's face in the rearview mirror. Mrs. Mota was staring back at Greg, and apparently she'd seen the whole thing.

Ten minutes later, Rick got off the bus carrying his backpack. Greg got off, too, but he was carrying a note from Mrs. Mota to the school principal. As Greg walked into the school, the expression on his face was pretty grim.

Name _____ Date _____

1. **When Rick grabs his backpack and sprints outside, you can predict that he is about to _____.**

Ⓐ go to school

Ⓑ run away from home

Ⓒ go to a friend's house

Ⓓ go for a long run

2. **The story says, "As he made his way to the only empty seat, Rick noticed Greg Ranier sitting across the aisle. Rick's stomach knotted up." What can you predict based on this information?**

_____

_____

3. **What probably happened next after Rick saw Mrs. Mota's face in the rearview mirror?**

Ⓐ Rick and Greg sat together.

Ⓑ Mrs. Mota started laughing.

Ⓒ Rick teased Greg.

Ⓓ Mrs. Mota spoke to Greg.

4. **What will Rick probably do next in the story?**

Ⓐ do his homework again

Ⓑ go to his classroom

Ⓒ talk to Greg's friends

Ⓓ take the bus home

5. **Write one or two sentences predicting what you think will happen to Greg in school.**

_____

_____

Name _____ Date _____

Directions: Read the passage. Then use the information from the passage to answer questions 1–5.

U.S. Immigration Today

Many people who live in the United States were not born here. They moved to the United States as children or adults. During the 1990s, about 1.3 million immigrants came to the United States every year. In 2000 and 2001, the number of immigrants grew. Today, new immigrants still come into the United States every day.

Before 1965, the United States set certain immigration quotas. The quotas limited the number of immigrants who could come from certain countries. In 1965, Congress decided to do away with the quotas. Since then, more than 60 percent of immigrants to the United States have come from Asia, Africa, Latin America, and the Middle East.

Airplane travel has also influenced immigration. In the 1800s and the early part of the 1900s, many people had to travel by boat to get to the United States. The trip was long and risky. Some people got sick or died on the way. The growth of air travel made it faster and easier to reach the United States from anywhere in the world. Today, people can travel quickly to the United States from distant countries such as Sudan or Vietnam. This has caused greater diversity, or variety, in the people who come to the United States.

Immigrants take risks to come here and work hard to succeed in their new home. They have helped the United States grow into a strong nation.

Name _____ Date _____

1. Which prediction could you make after reading the first paragraph?

Ⓐ   Immigrants will soon make up a very small percentage of the population of the United States.

Ⓑ   The United States will soon make laws to limit the number of new immigrants.

Ⓒ   Less than 1 million immigrants will come to the United States this year.

Ⓓ   At least 1.3 million new immigrants will come to the United States this year.

2. You can predict that an Asian immigrant coming to the United States today is most likely to arrive by _____.

Ⓐ   airplane

Ⓑ   boat

Ⓒ   train

Ⓓ   car

3. When poor immigrants come to the United States, what are they most likely to do first?

Ⓐ   buy homes

Ⓑ   vote in elections

Ⓒ   find jobs

Ⓓ   buy new clothes

4. If immigration quotas were still in place today, how might the population of the United States be different?

_____

_____

5. If the airplane had not been invented, how might immigration to the United States be different?

_____

_____

Name _____ Date _____

Directions: Read the passage. Then use the information from the passage to answer questions 1–5.

From Smoke Signals to Satellites

Long ago, people communicated from a distance in many ways. Some Native Americans used smoke signals to send messages. Some Africans beat drums. South Americans and Asians who lived near the ocean blew into seashells. People from many parts of the world have used stones, wood, or other objects to show directions. For example, when stones were stacked in a pile by a trail with one extra stone on the right or left, a traveler knew which way to turn.

For larger ideas, people needed new ways to communicate. Until the 1400s, books were slowly made by hand, one at a time. Around 1454 in Germany, Johannes Gutenberg printed the first book with a mechanical printing press. The press used movable type. With this press, many copies of the same book could be made faster and for less money. More and more people could buy and read books. As a result, ideas, information, and stories spread to people in all directions.

Printing books on paper was a major feat. The next breakthrough was getting rid of paper.

Telecommunications

Alexander Graham Bell was an early pioneer in communicating at a distance. He invented the first working telephone in 1876. In 1897, Guglielmo Marconi built the first wireless telegraph. Since then, technology has evolved at an amazing pace. Today, people page each other, send faxes, use cell phones, and send e-mail. Satellites in space receive signals from anywhere on Earth (and beyond). In an instant, they send the messages to other places.

Future Communications

How else might people communicate in the future? In 1998, Dr. Kevin Warwick tested an idea. He had tiny microchips placed in his arm for one week. A microchip can run computers. The microchips in his arm matched those in the building where he worked. When Dr. Warwick approached a door, the door opened. In the same way, his computer turned on. His hands never touched the objects.

How do you think you might send messages in the future?

Name _____ Date _____

1. **Long ago, people used drums, seashells, or smoke signals to _____.**
   Ⓐ eliminate the use of paper
   Ⓑ send messages to one another
   Ⓒ invent secret codes and languages
   Ⓓ find sources of food and water

2. **"When stones were stacked in a pile by a trail with one extra stone on the right or left, a traveler knew which way to turn." Rewrite this sentence in your own words.**

   _____

   _____

3. **What happened as a result of Gutenberg's invention of the printing press?**
   Ⓐ Books could be printed without paper.
   Ⓑ People immediately wanted to have telephones.
   Ⓒ Many people in different places could read the same books.
   Ⓓ Messages were sent instantly to distant places.

4. **Write a summary of this passage in one or two sentences.**

   _____

   _____

5. **Which sentence could be included in a summary of the Telecommunications section?**
   Ⓐ People have communicated from the beginning of time.
   Ⓑ Johannes Gutenberg printed the first book with his printing press around 1454.
   Ⓒ The future holds new ways to communicate.
   Ⓓ Alexander Graham Bell invented the telephone in 1876.

Name _____ Date _____

Directions: Read the passage. Then use the information from the passage to answer questions 1–5.

White House Animals

Presidents have lived in the White House for more than 200 years. In that time there have been many White House animals. The most common pets have been dogs and cats, as you would expect. But a few White House animals seem better suited to a barnyard than our country's grandest home.

Two of these animals were goats named Nanny and Nanko. They belonged to Abraham Lincoln's sons, Tad and Willie. Nanny and Nanko were allowed inside the White House, and the boys found ways to amuse themselves with the goats. They sometimes hitched the goats to carts and drove them through the White House. One time Nanko pulled Tad right into a fancy White House party!

President Theodore Roosevelt's six children had many pets. One was a pony named Algonquin. When young Archie Roosevelt was sick in bed, his brothers brought Algonquin to visit him. Getting the pony to Archie's second-floor bedroom wasn't difficult for the boys. They simply put Algonquin in the elevator and rode upstairs!

Probably the strangest White House animals ever were sheep. President Woodrow Wilson brought sheep to the White House during World War I. It was a time when everyone tried to save money to help pay for things our troops needed. Instead of paying workers to cut the White House lawn, President Wilson let the sheep graze there. What a funny sight that must have been!

White House Animals

Name _____ Date _____

1. Which is the best summary of the first paragraph?

Ⓐ   Most animals that have lived at the White House in the last 200 years
      have been dogs and cats. But there have been farm animals, too.

Ⓑ   Barnyard animals don't belong at the White House. It is too grand
      for animals like these.

Ⓒ   The White House has had many different kinds of animals. Dogs, cats,
      and other animals have been kept in a barnyard.

Ⓓ   Dogs and cats are not barnyard animals. Some dogs and cats
      have lived at the White House.

**2. The passage says, "Nanny and Nanko were allowed inside the White House,
    and the boys found ways to amuse themselves with the goats." Write a
    paraphrase of this sentence.**

_____

_____

3. Which of these sentences should be included in a summary of the third paragraph?

Ⓐ   Some White House animals include sheep, goats, and a pony.

Ⓑ   Both Lincoln and Roosevelt had young children while they were president.

Ⓒ   The Lincoln boys' pets were named Nanny and Nanko.

Ⓓ   The Roosevelt children once took their pony up a White House elevator.

**4. Which is the best paraphrase of this sentence? "Instead of paying workers to cut
    the White House lawn, President Wilson let the sheep graze there."**

Ⓐ   President Wilson saved money by using sheep instead of workers to cut the lawn.

Ⓑ   Workers are paid to cut the lawn where President Wilson's sheep used to graze.

Ⓒ   President Wilson thought workers could do other jobs while sheep kept the lawn cut.

Ⓓ   President Wilson thought sheep were better at keeping the lawn cut than the workers.

5. Write one or two sentences summarizing this passage.

_____

_____

_____

_____

Name _____ Date _____

Directions: Read the passage. Then use the information from the passage to answer questions 1–5.

Dorothea Lange: A Sensitive Eye

Dorothea Lange was a famous photographer. She is well known for her moving photos of the time period known as the Great Depression. It was one of the most trying times in U.S. history. For many years there were not enough jobs, and many people became very poor. Lange's photographs serve as a record of these hard times.

Dorothea Lange knew about personal hardship. When she was seven years old she caught polio. She walked with a limp for the rest of her life. When she was twelve, her father left the family.

At age 18, Lange decided to become a photographer. She began taking classes and working with other photographers. Later, she traveled throughout the country taking photos of people who were suffering the hardships of the Great Depression. She wanted to capture the toll that the Depression was taking on people. She first spent time talking to people to gain their trust. Then she would ask permission to photograph them. She tried to photograph them doing natural, ordinary things such as working, not posing stiffly for the camera.

One of her most famous photos is called "Migrant Mother." A migrant is someone who has to move from place to place to find work. The photo shows a tired-looking young woman. She is holding two small children who are hiding their faces. This touching photo became a symbol of the Great Depression.

Today Lange's work hangs in museums all over the world. Her photos are like living records of the brave people who survived bad times.

Progress-Monitoring Comprehension Strategy Assessments ⑥

Name _____ Date _____

1. **Which sentence best summarizes the information in the first paragraph?**
   - Ⓐ Lange lived during the Great Depression.
   - Ⓑ Lange was a sensitive photographer.
   - Ⓒ Lange was a famous photographer who recorded the Great Depression.
   - Ⓓ Lange found it difficult to become a photographer during the Great Depression.

2. **The passage says, "It was one of the most trying times in U.S. history. For many years there were not enough jobs, and many people became very poor." Which is the best paraphrase of these two sentences?**
   - Ⓐ There were not enough jobs at this time in U.S. history, which was very poor.
   - Ⓑ Many people were not trying at this time in U.S. history and became very poor.
   - Ⓒ There were not enough jobs for people who became poor at this time in history.
   - Ⓓ In this difficult time, many people could not get jobs and became very poor.

3. **In your own words, write a summary of the information in the third paragraph.**

   _____

   _____

4. **In your own words, write a summary of the information in the fourth paragraph.**

   _____

   _____

5. **The passage says, "Today Lange's work hangs in museums all over the world. Her photos are like living records of the brave people who survived bad times." Which is the best paraphrase of these two sentences?**
   - Ⓐ Today Lange's work is kept by brave people all over the world.
   - Ⓑ Brave people visit museums all over the world to see Lange's work.
   - Ⓒ Lange's photos now serve as records of brave people and hard times.
   - Ⓓ Her photos prove that Lange survived bad times in museums.

Name _____ Date _____

Directions: Read the passage. Then use the information from the passage to answer questions 1–5.

What's That Sound?

The human ear is a remarkable organ. It is like a machine that collects sounds and sends them to your brain. Sound travels at about 760 miles per hour, so your ear has to function quickly. This is how it works.

Have you ever seen the way a funnel is used to pour liquid into something with a small opening? Your outer ear works like a funnel. It catches sound waves and "pours" them into your middle ear. The sound waves travel along until they strike the eardrum, which is a tightly stretched piece of skin. The sound waves cause the eardrum to vibrate, or move back and forth quickly, like the drum a musician plays in a band. The vibrating eardrum in turn causes vibrations in the ossicles. These are tiny bones in your middle ear.

Beyond the ossicles in the inner ear is the cochlea. This is a spiral-shaped tube filled with fluid and lined with tiny hairs. The vibrating ossicles cause the fluid, as well as the tiny hairs, to move around. The tiny hairs are attached to nerves, which then send messages to your brain. Your brain figures out what these sounds are. If your ear was not connected to your brain, you might feel vibrations from the sound waves, but you would not understand what the sounds mean.

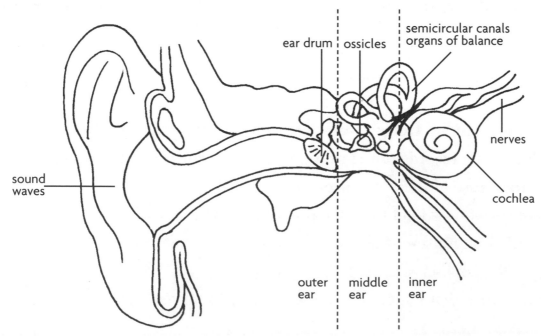

What's That Sound?

Name _____ Date _____

1. **Based on the labeled diagram, which sentence best describes how the ear works?**
   (A) The funnel is a wonderful tool. It is very much like an ear.
   (B) Sound travels from the outer ear through the middle ear and inner ear to the brain.
   (C) The ear contains an eardrum and many other parts.
   (D) The eardrum, ossicles, and cochlea all end up vibrating.

2. **What shape is the cochlea?**

   _____

3. **Which of these is the smallest?**
   (A) eardrum
   (B) ossicles
   (C) cochlea
   (D) outer ear

4. **Name two parts that are in the inner ear.**

   _____

   _____

5. **The "semicircular canals" in the middle ear help the body to _____.**
   (A) hear sounds from far away
   (B) regulate the brain
   (C) keep the ear passage clean
   (D) maintain balance

Name _____ Date _____

Directions: Read the passage. Then use the information from the passage to answer questions 1–5.

The Chain of Life

Although it might strike you as a strange concept, you are a link in a chain. This chain is made up of large animals, like you, the smaller animals that they (and you) eat, and the plants that those smaller animals eat. You've probably guessed that this chain is the food chain.

Food chains exist in all kinds of habitats. There are food chains in oceans, lakes, and rivers. There are food chains in rain forests and on grassy plains. Wherever plants and animals live and grow, there are food chains.

Let's use an ocean habitat to discover how a food chain works. The first link is made up of ocean plants. The second link includes the tiny fish that feed on these plants. These tiny fish are food for larger fish, such as tuna and swordfish. What eats these larger fish? Sharks and dolphins do, and so do many people! It is our need for food that links us to these ocean creatures and plants.

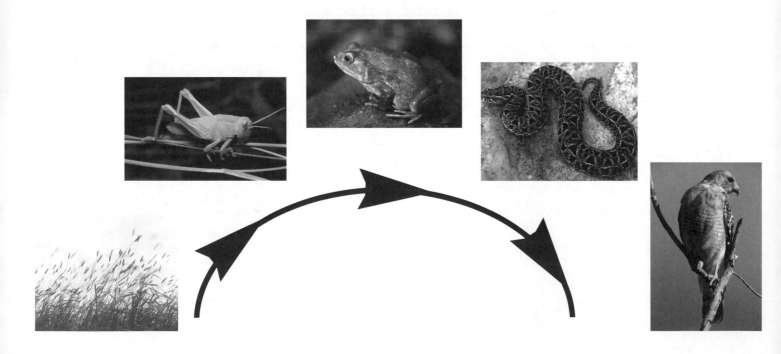

Name _____ Date _____

1. Which creature is the highest link on the food chain shown in the pictures?

Ⓐ   snake

Ⓑ   toad

Ⓒ   grasshopper

Ⓓ   hawk

2. What does a snake eat?

Ⓐ   toads

Ⓑ   baby hawks

Ⓒ   grasshoppers

Ⓓ   smaller snakes

3. Which creature is eaten by a toad?

_____

_____

4. Which creature on this food chain does not eat another creature?

Ⓐ   toad

Ⓑ   snake

Ⓒ   grasshopper

Ⓓ   hawk

5. Use this food chain to explain why grasshoppers are important to hawks.

_____

_____

Name _____ Date _____

Directions: Read the passage. Then use the information from the passage to answer questions 1–5.

The Picture of Health

It is not easy to know what to eat to stay healthy, or how much of each kind of food to eat. That's why the U.S. Department of Agriculture wants to help people understand healthful eating. One of the best ways to understand information is through pictures, so the department created the Food Guide Pyramid.

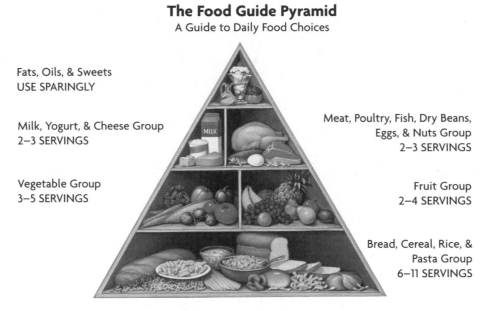

The Food Guide Pyramid
A Guide to Daily Food Choices

Fats, Oils, & Sweets
USE SPARINGLY

Milk, Yogurt, & Cheese Group
2–3 SERVINGS

Vegetable Group
3–5 SERVINGS

Meat, Poultry, Fish, Dry Beans,
Eggs, & Nuts Group
2–3 SERVINGS

Fruit Group
2–4 SERVINGS

Bread, Cereal, Rice, &
Pasta Group
6–11 SERVINGS

The Food Guide Pyramid doesn't tell you exactly which foods are best. For example, it does not tell you to eat hamburgers one day and chicken the next. But it does tell you what kinds of foods to eat. To stay healthy, you need to eat a lot of some foods and not very much of others. The ones you need the most of are at the bottom of the chart, and the ones you need less of are at the top.

The recommended number of servings of each kind of food is given as a range, such as two to four servings of fruit a day. It is a range because different people need different amounts of food. A six-foot-tall athlete needs more fuel than a five-foot-tall office worker.

By studying and using the Food Guide Pyramid, people can follow a healthful diet and enjoy what they eat.

The Picture of Health

Name _____ Date _____

1. **According to the Food Guide Pyramid, which kind of food should people eat the most of each day?**
   - (A) fats, oils, and sweets
   - (B) vegetables
   - (C) meat, poultry, fish, beans, eggs, and nuts
   - (D) bread, cereal, rice, and pasta

2. **According to the pyramid, how many servings of milk, yogurt, or cheese should people eat each day?**
   - (A) 2–3
   - (B) 3–5
   - (C) 5–7
   - (D) 6–11

3. **Jolene has a sandwich of peanut butter on whole wheat bread. Which two food groups does this sandwich fit into?**

   _____

   _____

4. **What is shown at the top of the Food Guide Pyramid?**

   _____

   _____

5. **Based on the number of servings daily, which is the second most important food group?**
   - (A) milk, yogurt, and cheese group
   - (B) meat and poultry group
   - (C) vegetable group
   - (D) fats, oils, and sweets group

Name _____ Date _____

Directions: Read the passage. Then use the information from the passage to answer questions 1–5.

Old Man River

The largest river in North America is the Mississippi River. It is sometimes called "Old Man River" or "Big Muddy." Ships, barges, and tugboats move up and down the river. They carry raw materials, agricultural goods, and other products.

Source

The mighty Mississippi River starts as a stream flowing out of **Lake Itasca** in Minnesota. From there, the river flows 2,340 miles (3,765 kilometers) to empty into the **Gulf of Mexico**. At its widest point in Clinton, Iowa, the river is 3.5 miles (5.6 kilometers) wide. Its depth ranges from 9 feet (2.7 meters) to 100 feet (30 meters). As it approaches the gulf, the river slows down. Just south of New Orleans, Louisiana, is the mouth of the river.

History

The first European explorer to see the Mississippi River was **Hernando de Soto** in 1541. In 1682, the French explorer **René Robert La Salle** claimed the entire Mississippi River Valley for France. The United States bought the valley and the river from France in 1803. The Mississippi became an important supply route for settlers moving to the West in the 1800s. It was also a key transportation route between the North and the South during the Civil War.

Name _____ Date _____

1. **In which part of the passage should you look to find out how long the Mississippi River is?**

   (A) first paragraph

   (B) **Source**

   (C) **History**

   (D) the map

2. **What is the source of the Mississippi River?**

   (A) Lake Itasca

   (B) Gulf of Mexico

   (C) Red River

   (D) New Orleans, Louisiana

3. **In which part of the passage should you look to find out who the first French explorer of the Mississippi River was?**

   (A) first paragraph

   (B) **Source**

   (C) **History**

   (D) the map

4. **Explain why the Mississippi River was an important waterway in the 1800s.**

   _____

   _____

5. **Who was Hernando de Soto, and what did he do?**

   _____

   _____

Name _____ Date _____

Directions: Read the passage. Then use the information from the passage to answer questions 1–5.

Herbert Elementary School
Fifth Grade News and Notes
— Week of May 2-6 —

We have just one more month of school, and everyone is looking forward to summer. But our fifth graders are as busy as ever! Here's some news about what's been happening, and what's coming up.

We've Been Learning:

Reading	What makes science fiction special?
Writing	How do you write a description?
Math	How are graphs used to show information?
Science	What do plants need to grow?
Social Studies	Who were the first Americans?

Dates to Remember:

May 9   **Gardening Day:** We will plant flowers outside the front doors of the school. Students should wear old clothes, a hat, and sunscreen.

May 13   **Field Trip:** We will take an all-day trip to the Colonial Village in Lewisburg. Students should bring a bag lunch and a snack. The bus will leave at 9:15 A.M. and return by 2:50 P.M.

May 18   **Middle School Visit:** Students will visit Blair Middle School from 12:30 P.M. to 2:30 P.M. They will meet the principal and visit some classrooms. Important Reminder: We will be walking to and from Blair Middle School. Students should wear comfortable shoes and dress for the weather!

May 21   **School Fair:** Come for the games and prizes, or come for the music and great food. Just make sure you come! The fair will be held from 4:00 to 8:00 P.M. on the playground.

Name _____ Date _____

1. What school do the fifth graders attend?

_____

_____

2. On what day will the students take a field trip?

Ⓐ　May 6

Ⓑ　May 13

Ⓒ　May 18

Ⓓ　May 21

3. What have the students been doing in science class?

Ⓐ　reading science fiction

Ⓑ　making and using graphs

Ⓒ　learning how plants grow

Ⓓ　learning about the weather

4. What will the students do on May 9?

Ⓐ　plant flowers

Ⓑ　visit Colonial Village

Ⓒ　take a walk

Ⓓ　have a school fair

5. What important reminder is included in the information about the middle school visit?

_____

_____

Name _____ Date _____

Directions: Read the passage. Then use the information from the passage to answer questions 1–5.

Workers with Wings

Bees have stingers, and they often seem to land where they're not wanted. So why would anybody actually want to raise bees in *hives*? There are several reasons.

Honey Machines

The biggest reason for keeping bees is for the honey they make. Honey is a delicious sweet treat, sometimes called "the perfect food" because it never spoils. Bees make honey from *nectar*, which is a kind of sweet juice that comes from flowers. The bees make honey as food for the winter, and they store it in *honeycombs*.

Flower Helpers

Bees go from flower to flower in their search for nectar. As they do so, traces of powdery *pollen* stick to their legs. Each time a bee lands on a new flower, a little pollen from other flowers comes off. That is how flowers are *pollinated*. Without the bees, there wouldn't be nearly as many flowers. The blossoms need to be pollinated to make flowers for next year.

Candle Makers

When bees make honey, they store it in honeycombs made of wax. Bees make the wax with glands in their bodies. Beeswax is used to make the very best candles, which burn for a long time and smell like honey.

Health Food

Bees also make something called *propolis*, which is a mixture of wax and resins. The bees use this to seal up the cells of their honeycombs. Many people believe that it is a health food, so they eat it to combat colds and other illnesses.

Bees may be small, but they do many things that help people. It is surprising there aren't more hives in America's backyards!

Workers with Wings

Name _____ Date _____

1. In which part of this passage can you find information about beeswax?
   (A) Honey Machines
   (B) Flower Helpers
   (C) Candle Makers
   (D) Health Food

2. According to this passage, what is nectar?
   (A) the perfect food
   (B) a powder from flowers
   (C) a mixture of wax and resins
   (D) a juice from flowers

3. Under which heading should you look for information about pollen?
   (A) Honey Machines
   (B) Flower Helpers
   (C) Candle Makers
   (D) Health Food

4. What do bees use honeycombs for?

   _____

   _____

5. According to this passage, why do some people eat propolis?

   _____

   _____

Answer Key

Analyze Character
Grade 5
Rather Retires
1. B
2. D
3. A
4. Example: He felt tied down. He missed being in the field.
5. He believes news should be reported from the middle of the action so people can see what's happening. He once tied himself to a tree to report on a hurricane.

The "No Pets" Problem
1. C
2. D
3. A
4. Examples: He likes and respects his grandfather. He listens to him and obeys his instructions. He enjoys the activities he and his grandfather do together.
5. Example: He could pick up a turtle and hold it.

Grade 6
A Hero for Working People
1. B
2. C
3. Example: He and his friends had no rights and no say in their jobs.
4. A
5. Example: He won the Nobel Peace Prize and suddenly became famous all over the world.

Analyze Story Elements
Grade 5
Making Yippee
1. D
2. C
3. A
4. Example: The sun came out on Sun Day.
5. Example: She had made a new friend, and there were only 49 days left.

Double Take
1. A
2. C
3. D
4. Example: Edwin bumped into Sally while they were both looking at photographs, and Felix noticed Edwin.
5. Example: They were going to talk to Felix's parents about what they had discovered, or ask some questions.

Grade 6
The Happy Camper
1. B
2. Example: It is morning at a campground in the woods.
3. B
4. A
5. Example: Juanita goes from being grumpy to happy or excited when she sees a milk snake (and teases Caroline).

Analyze Text Structure and Organization
Grade 5
Getting Energy from the Sun
1. D
2. B
3. A
4. Example: when gas bubbles burst on the surface of the sun
5. Example: to call attention to important words

Robot Cars Aren't Up to the Challenge
1. C
2. B
3. B
4. Example: The author describes what the Challenge course involves and how the race will proceed.
5. Example: to describe what happened to the bots or to tell how they failed

Grade 6
Music from Steam
1. C
2. A
3. B
4. Example: on steamboats or in circuses
5. Example: There are only 14 calliopes left. A few steamboats still have them.

Answer Key

Compare and Contrast
Grade 5
Elephant Songs
1. C
2. D
3. A
4. Examples: They send warning calls, tell about food, ask for help, and give mating calls.
5. Examples: She discovered that elephants use low-frequency sounds to communicate.

Kayaks
1. D
2. C
3. B
4. Example: They are stretched along the top of the kayak and are used to hold tools or supplies in place.
5. Examples: Today's kayaks are made of plastic or fiberglass; they are heavier; they have spray skirts and metal or plastic paddles.

Grade 6
Are Hybrid Cars Safe?
1. B
2. Example: Hybrid cars have an electric motor and regular cars do not.
3. C
4. a contrast; the author tells how the batteries are different
5. A

Draw Conclusions
Grade 5
Etna Blows Its Top
1. C
2. Example: The eruption of Mount Etna made the area unsafe.
3. A
4. D
5. Example: They are used to it and do not seem too worried about it. The people still live near Mount Etna and grow crops on the mountainside.

Solving Problems
1. B
2. Example: Calvin thinks Danita has some excellent ideas about what she would do.
3. A
4. Example: He decides to tell Sonya the truth about what he is thinking instead of voting for her or keeping his vote a secret.
5. C

Grade 6
Let's Take a Closer Look
1. C
2. A
3. D
4. Example: Without his work, we might not have the medical knowledge we have today.
5. Example: Microscopes led to important medical discoveries. Much of what we know today about curing disease we learned from using microscopes.

Evaluate Author's Purpose and Point of View
Grade 5
Two Sisters
1. Example: to give information about the Delany sisters
2. B
3. "Both sisters certainly had long and exciting lives."
4. D
5. C

Pigs or Plants?
1. A
2. C
3. C
4. Example: to make the pig problem seem even more serious
5. Example: The author gives information about the pigs' negative impact on native plants. She says that in order to save many native plants and animals, the pigs must go.

Grade 6
Island of Mystery/Ecology of an Island
1. A
2. C
3. B
4. Examples: why the statues were built; what the writing on the stone tablets means; where the first people on Easter Island came from
5. Example: The author thinks the people were foolish, stupid, shortsighted, or irresponsible for cutting down the trees.

Answer Key

Evaluate Fact and Opinion
Grade 5
Two Native American Peoples: The Iroquois and the Zuni
1. C
2. C
3. Example: Fifty male chiefs, or sachems, ruled the Iroquois League. This is a fact because it can be verified.
4. Example: Zuni women made beautiful clay pots. This is an opinion because it expresses a personal belief.
5. A

Having It Both Ways
1. D
2. C
3. D
4. Example: "Customers were eating more than one million a day!" This is a fact because it can be verified.
5. Example: "That little boy who could not make up his mind was a great help, too." This is an opinion because it expresses a personal belief.

Grade 6
A Monument to the Country
1. B
2. C
3. Example: "The government's actions were shameful."
4. Example: "Mount Rushmore stands in the Black Hills of South Dakota."
5. D

Identify Cause and Effect
Grade 5
Amphibian Population Declining: Scientists Concerned
1. C
2. A
3. D
4. Example: It destroys their habitat and leaves them with no place to live.
5. Example: A problem with amphibians may be a warning sign of problems that will affect other species, including people.

Explaining Earthquakes
1. A
2. C
3. D
4. Example: It releases energy and makes the ground shake.
5. Examples: mud or rock slides, volcanoes, and tsunamis

Grade 6
Mount St. Helens
1. D
2. C
3. Example: It had received scientific reports about Mount St. Helens ahead of time.
4. A
5. Example: so they can learn about how plants and animals respond after the land is destroyed by a volcano.

Identify Main Idea and Supporting Details
Grade 5
Picture This!
1. C
2. A
3. Example: The flashbulb was first used in 1925.
4. Example: Louis Daguerre made it possible to preserve images of people, places, and events.
5. C

Mollusks
1. B
2. D
3. Example: Mollusks make their own shells by oozing layers of lime.
4. Example: When they die, many of them leave behind beautiful shells.
5. C

Grade 6
Time Zones
1. B
2. Example: The sun rises later in California than it does in New York.
3. Example: Before 1883, each city or town decided on its own time.
4. D
5. A

Answer Key

Identify Sequence or Steps in a Process
Grade 5

An Experiment with Light
1. Example: Hold the glass away from the window.
2. C
3. Example: Hold a white paper under the rainbow.
4. B
5. D

Ben Franklin
1. B
2. Example: He worked as an apprentice in his brother James's printing shop.
3. C
4. A
5. Example: He invented the lightning rod.

Grade 6

Westward We Go!
1. C
2. A
3. Example: because the animals pulled the wagons
4. B
5. Example: They needed fuel to make the cooking fire.

Make Inferences
Grade 5

A New Fin for Fuji
1. B
2. D
3. Example: to swim fast and to jump out of the water
4. A
5. Example: Rubber is waterproof and flexible in the water, just like a dolphin's fin. It can be cut to just the right shape and size.

The Statue of Helios
1. A
2. Example: The statue took a long time to build because it was so huge, or because it was cast of metal.
3. C
4. B
5. Example: The people feared the power Helios had over their lives. They built the statue to show respect and thanks, but when they believed Helios struck It down, they were afraid to rebuild it.

Grade 6

Where the Buffalo Roam
1. B
2. D
3. Example: People have been trying to increase the number of buffalo.
4. A
5. Example: They might feel that their concerns about their cattle are more important than protecting history.

Make Judgments
Grade 5

Mushrooms
1. Example: Fairy ring mushrooms probably taste best because they are used to flavor soups.
2. B
3. D
4. B
5. Example: Many kinds of fungi are poisonous, and many are very difficult to identify.

Reconstruction
1. C
2. B
3. C
4. Example: He would have been upset or discouraged because the country was still divided in many ways.
5. Examples: He wanted the North and South to be one nation again. He made the South free all the slaves and return to the Union. He wanted the South to rebuild.

Grade 6

Astronauts
1. A
2. C
3. D
4. Example: It promotes the application process as if it were an adventurous vacation.
5. Example: Yes, because people who are in less than perfect health can become very ill from space travel.

Answer Key

Make Predictions
Grade 5

An Afternoon in Wilmington
1. C
2. B
3. Example: Someone would investigate and find a runaway slave hidden in the hay, or the farmer would drive quickly away.
4. Examples: William would tell his father about what happened, or the slave in the hay wagon would escape.
5. A

On the Bus
1. A
2. Example: There will be trouble between Rick and Greg.
3. D
4. B
5. Example: He will bring the note to the principal and will have to explain that he was bothering Rick. He may have to apologize to Rick or stay in at recess.

Grade 6

U.S. Immigration Today
1. D
2. A
3. C
4. Example: There would be fewer immigrants from Asia, Africa, Latin America, and the Middle East.
5. Example: There would be less diversity because fewer people would come from distant countries.

Summarize Information
Grade 5

From Smoke Signals to Satellites
1. B
2. Example: Piles of stones were placed by the trail to give directions for travelers.
3. C
4. Example: Communications have changed a lot over the centuries, from the first printing press to the most modern microchips.
5. D

White House Animals
1. A
2. Example: The boys had fun with their goats inside the White House.
3. D
4. A
5. Example: Some barnyard animals have lived at the White House. They included Lincoln's goats, Theodore Roosevelt's pony, and Wilson's sheep.

Grade 6

Dorothea Lange: A Sensitive Eye
1. C
2. D
3. Example: Lange photographed poor people all over the country. She won their trust and got their permission first. She tried to capture people while they were working or doing regular things.
4. Example: Lange's most famous photograph, "Migrant Mother," became a symbol of the Great Depression. It shows a mother holding two small children.
5. C

Use Graphic Features to Interpret Information
Grade 5

What's That Sound?
1. B
2. Example: It is round, or spiral-shaped.
3. B
4. cochlea and nerves
5. D

The Chain of Life
1. D
2. A
3. grasshoppers
4. C
5. Examples: Without grasshoppers, hawks would go hungry. Grasshoppers are food for toads, which are food for snakes, and hawks eat snakes.

Grade 6

The Picture of Health
1. D
2. A
3. Example: the bread group and the meat group
4. Example: the fats, oils, and sweets are shown at the top of the pyramid.
5. C

Answer Key

Use Text Features to Locate Information
Grade 5
Old Man River
1. B
2. A
3. C
4. Example: It was an important supply route for settlers moving west and a transportation route between the North and South during the Civil War.
5. He was the first European explorer to see the Mississippi River.

Herbert Elementary School
Fifth Grade News and Notes
1. Herbert Elementary School
2. B
3. C
4. A
5. Example: The students are going to walk to the middle school and back. They need to wear comfortable shoes and the right clothes for the weather.

Grade 6
Workers with Wings
1. C
2. D
3. B
4. Example: They store honey in honeycombs for the winter.
5. Example: They think it is a health food; they eat it to fight colds and diseases.

Scoring Chart

Student Name _____ Grade _____

Strategy	Test 1 Date / Score	Test 2 Date / Score	Test 3 Date / Score	Notes
Analyze Character	Date: _____ / 5	Date: _____ / 5	Date: _____ / 5	
Analyze Story Elements	Date: _____ / 5	Date: _____ / 5	Date: _____ / 5	
Analyze Text Structure and Organization	Date: _____ / 5	Date: _____ / 5	Date: _____ / 5	
Compare and Contrast	Date: _____ / 5	Date: _____ / 5	Date: _____ / 5	
Draw Conclusions	Date: _____ / 5	Date: _____ / 5	Date: _____ / 5	
Evaluate Author's Purpose and Point of View	Date: _____ / 5	Date: _____ / 5	Date: _____ / 5	
Evaluate Fact and Opinion	Date: _____ / 5	Date: _____ / 5	Date: _____ / 5	
Identify Cause and Effect	Date: _____ / 5	Date: _____ / 5	Date: _____ / 5	
Identify Main Idea and Supporting Details	Date: _____ / 5	Date: _____ / 5	Date: _____ / 5	
Identify Sequence or Steps in a Process	Date: _____ / 5	Date: _____ / 5	Date: _____ / 5	
Make Inferences	Date: _____ / 5	Date: _____ / 5	Date: _____ / 5	
Make Judgments	Date: _____ / 5	Date: _____ / 5	Date: _____ / 5	
Make Predictions	Date: _____ / 5	Date: _____ / 5	Date: _____ / 5	
Summarize Information	Date: _____ / 5	Date: _____ / 5	Date: _____ / 5	
Use Graphic Features to Interpret Information	Date: _____ / 5	Date: _____ / 5	Date: _____ / 5	
Use Text Features to Locate Information	Date: _____ / 5	Date: _____ / 5	Date: _____ / 5	

Notes